THINK OUTSIDE THE TEXTBOOK

REAL TALK FOR REAL LIFE SUCCESS

SCOTT GRATES

Think Outside the Textbook: Real Talk for Real-Life Success
Copyright © 2024 Scott Grates

No part of this book may be reproduced or transmitted in any form or by any means, electronic or mechanical, including photocopying and recording, or by any information storage or retrieval system, except as may be expressly permitted by the 1976 Copyright Act or in writing from the publisher. Requests for permission should be addressed to storybuilderspress@gmail.com.

Published by StoryBuilders Press.

978-1-954521-73-5 eBook
978-1-954521-74-2 Paperback

DEDICATION

To my son, Conner—your hard work, character, and kindness have inspired me more than you'll ever know. As you step into the next chapter of your life, this book is my gift to you—a road map to help you navigate the world with confidence and purpose. Be bold, be brave, and always be YOU.

TABLE OF CONTENTS

CHAPTER ONE Welcome to Your Next Adventure 7

CHAPTER TWO Warning: Self-Imposed Limits 24

CHAPTER THREE Better Thoughts Beyond This Point 45

CHAPTER FOUR No Turning Back 64

CHAPTER FIVE Watch for Inner Work Opportunities 82

CHAPTER SIX Fuel for the Journey 101

CHAPTER SEVEN No Stopping You Now 118

CHAPTER EIGHT Seeding the Path 134

CHAPTER NINE Bright Future Ahead 152

Acknowledgments 172
About the Author 173

CHAPTER ONE

WELCOME TO YOUR NEXT ADVENTURE

*When you come to a fork
in the road, take it.*
—YOGI BERRA

A t some point in your life, you will find yourself transitioning from school to whatever is next, whether it's from high school to college, a trade school, graduate school, or making the decision to drop out—it doesn't matter what you're moving from. You need to understand (and most likely, you already know this, but it bears repeating) that schools are pretty good at teaching you *what* to think, but they aren't as good at teaching you *how* to think. And that's where I'd like to step in and give you a hand on the next phase of your life as you figure out what adventure you want to take.

My mission is to help you by sharing the real-world knowledge I've gained through lived experience as the person who continued to ask, "Why do I have to do it that way?" and "Is there a better way to look at this?" This book contains the pieces of advice I wish I had back when I started my journey into adulthood. And now I get to pay it forward by giving you a resource I needed when I was just starting out in the real world.

Albert Einstein is often attributed with saying, "Everybody is a genius. But if you judge a fish by its ability to climb a tree, it will live its whole life believing that it is stupid." I wasn't stupid as a high schooler, but I didn't realize it for a while. I didn't give a crap about math, science, history, or any of the required curriculum that my teachers tried to force-feed me. During my junior year of high school, my road forward was to apply to work in a nearby factory after graduation. Minimum wage at the time was five dollars an hour. They were paying fifteen, and that sounded just fine to me.

However, with the support of some incredible coaches and strong mentors, going to college felt like it could be an option after all. I'll admit, it was a struggle at first because my study habits were pretty nonexistent. But once I found myself finally enjoying the content, I flourished. I made the dean's list, and I got into personal development—I loved that stuff! I couldn't get enough of it. I had found the direction I wanted to take my adventure.

Maybe you aren't (or weren't) the best stereotypical high school student. Maybe you don't know which direction you want to take at this point in your life. But take comfort in knowing that many people (myself included) were once where you are now—doubting your abilities, selling yourself short, worrying a lot about everything. But just like my younger self, you have a ton of potential just waiting for you to tap into it!

So think of me as the wise older character who shows up from the future with insight on your next twenty-five years. I lived through all the things you're about to face on this next adventure, and there are certain things—forks in the road—that are absolutely, positively going to show up along the way and will require you to make a choice.

New York Yankees pitcher Yogi Berra once famously said, "When you come to a fork in the road, take it." Yogi gave these instructions to his friend and fellow MLB catcher, Joe Garagiola, when telling Joe how to get to his house in Montclair, New Jersey. At first glance, these directions might sound about as clear as mud.

The road goes in two directions. Where am I supposed to go?

But the irony is that both sides of the fork in the road actually led to Yogi's home. You couldn't have seen it from the fork, but *there wasn't one right and one wrong path to take.*

As you're figuring out your own direction, the refreshing twist is that it's often the same way with life. I'm not here to tell you what to do. Life is a game, and you get to choose your own adventure. Once you finish high school, you're on free play. The options are endless. You can walk down many possible roads—different cities, careers, relationships, opportunities. But it's not as if there's one *right* road that you need to worry about missing.

What I can do is share what I've learned to help you know how to think about those decisions. School taught you what to think; it's time to learn *how*. Once you do, you'll understand yourself and what you want out of life a little better—and you'll be able to make the moves that resonate with your values when the time comes. Sounds pretty good, right?

ALLOW ME TO BE YOUR CONTRARIAN GUIDE

In the 1950s, a psychologist named Dr. Solomon Asch conducted a series of experiments to see how majority viewpoints influenced individuals' beliefs and opinions. The results were astounding. And they've influenced the way we've understood conformity and peer pressure ever since.

The experiment consisted of giving participants one card with a single line on it and a second card with three lines, labeled *A*, *B*, and *C*. One of the lines on the second card was identical to that on the first, while each of the other two were clearly shorter or longer. Participants were simply asked to identify which lines matched.

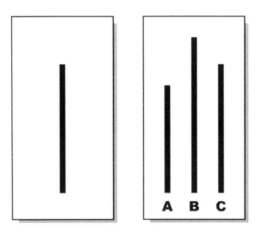

Asch placed the participants in groups of eight, having one uninformed participant paired with seven actors who were in on the experiment. Asch had the actors give correct answers to a few initial questions but then had them begin to uniformly answer the questions incorrectly to see how peer pressure affected the one unwitting participant in each group.

In the end, over a third of test subjects conformed to giving a wrong answer at least once—even when the correct answer was seemingly obvious. When interviewed, many of these participants told Asch that they *really believed* the wrong answer was the right one. Their view of reality had been distorted by popular influence. When asked what he thought about the results, Asch commented, "That intelligent, well-meaning young people are willing to call white black is a matter of concern."

Asch's experiments demonstrate the importance of being able to think for yourself and to adopt a contrarian perspective when necessary. Especially in today's digitally dominated world, people can quickly become copy-and-paste. Rather than be original, they steal their ideas from AI. Instead of critically thinking, they hop on whatever is virally trending. *It's all too easy to let others do your thinking for you.*

So how are you going to be unique? How are you going to stand out? There are upwards of twenty thousand high schools in the United States today. That means there will be more than twenty thousand graduating classes with more than twenty thousand valedictorians this year alone.

However, the metric for determining success in the classroom hardly translates to a metric for success in the real world. The only thing standardized tests can really capture is your ability to absorb content and retain it long enough to regurgitate it on the test. And sure, that requires a lot of time and hard work. But what I'm looking for as an employer (and what most employers are looking for) is what you did *that you didn't have to do*. What is it that makes you different from everyone else?

If you want exceptional results, you can't just do what everyone else is doing. Think about it. Anyone you idolize—

anyone you look up to as a mentor or a hero—is someone who had the courage *to think differently*. Otherwise, they would just be like everyone else: copy-and-paste.

Henry Ford, the great captain of industry who developed the automobile assembly line, is often attributed with saying, "If I had asked people what they wanted, they would have said faster horses." Without questioning the common way of doing things—without thinking outside the box—Ford never would have innovated in the way he did to revolutionize the automobile industry. So why not try to "reinvent the wheel"? It might just lead to the next big thing.

Taking on a contrarian view is better than just getting an answer and running with it. When you see the masses heading in one direction, look the other way and question, *Why is everyone going that way?*

Question everything. Don't ask questions looking for an answer, but ask questions to obtain new wisdom. You don't have to do everything differently just for the sake of being different. But when you are willing to look for different answers—to take that bold risk—the rewards can be much greater and more fulfilling than if you had played it safe.

GET STUPID

As a business owner myself, I wholeheartedly believe that this is the greatest time in the history of our planet to be alive as a young person, at least as far as opportunities and advantages go. The old-school ways of "Who do you know?"; "Where do you come from?"; "What college can you get into?" have fallen by the wayside.

Today nearly 70 percent of American billionaires are self-made. And more than half of all entrepreneurs—the majority of small business owners—never got a college degree. In a world where information flows freely, you can give yourself the knowledge to succeed just by listening to the right podcasts and reading the right books. The amount of opportunities these days for people who take initiative and do the little things that have a huge impact is truly unlimited.

During my career, I was told that goals should be SMART: Specific, Measurable, Attainable, Realistic, and with a Timeline. I'm not saying it's a bad formula, but I am telling you that it's a boring approach that challenges you to play small. Take on that contrarian mindset. Again, you're not going to have exceptional results unless you think a little differently from everyone else.

There is a place for SMART goals, but I'm going to challenge you to challenge yourself to dream bigger. So big that people laugh at you, tell you you're crazy, and even think to themselves, *That's stupid*. And they'd be right!

However, they wouldn't realize you are following the STUPID acronym, going after your Scary, Teachable, Unbelievable, Positive, and Impactful Dreams. Let's dive into why it makes more sense to be STUPID.

- ○ **S**—Scary
- ○ **T**—Teachable
- ○ **U**—Unbelievable
- ○ **P**—Positive
- ○ **I**—Impactful
- ○ **D**—Dream

1. **SCARY:** If something doesn't challenge you, it will never change you. All change is scary. Big changes are especially scary because your likelihood of failure increases. Remember, it's that fear of failure which sits at the core of why we don't pursue bigger dreams. Step 1 in this process is to set a goal so big that the mere thought of it gives you butterflies.

   Having a STUPID goal requires you to be challenged—that you make room for new and big ideas. New ideas might feel scary because you currently lack the knowledge or experience required to execute them. However, knowledge can be taught, which is why it's important for you to also be teachable.

2. **TEACHABLE:** Can you teach yourself or surround yourself with others who can teach you how to make your goal a reality? The answer is *yes*. It's all too easy to waste your time doom-scrolling through TikTok and Instagram, filling your head with brainless content. Let me challenge you to make the switch to absorb content that will grow and benefit you—even if it's just for twenty minutes each day.

   Become a knowledge junkie, and take every free minute to consume the information you need to accomplish your desired goal. Try searching for podcasts from thought leaders on the topic you're interested in. Buy a popular book or two on the subject. If you don't know where to begin, you could even use Google or AI to find articles that will help you get your feet wet. The more you learn, the less intimidating it will feel.

Soon, you will also learn that it's *who*, not just *how*. To gain real-world insight and experience, research people already working in the area of your goal. Proactively send them a letter or email (though emails are less personal and more likely to get ignored). Introduce yourself and why you are interested in their work, and let them know that you hope to meet one day. Follow them on social media, build your LinkedIn profile, and make your aspirations clear. As opportunities arise for internships or job shadowing, you will already be known to the people you want to connect with and learn from.

3. **UNBELIEVABLE:** If you told a friend in 1869 that we'd put a human being on the moon in 1969, they would never believe it. If you told a caveman dependent on fire that one day we'd flip a switch and light an entire room, he'd never believe you. If you told me when I was in grade school that I could type a few words onto a computer and instantly have endless information on that subject—thanks, Google and AI—I'd never believe you. My point is, nothing was ever believable before it became a reality. Is your goal something that nine out of ten people wouldn't believe is possible? If so, you're on the right track!

4. **POSITIVE AND IMPACTFUL:** I will cover the positive and impactful pieces together. Will your goal make a positive impact on the world? Is it a solution to a problem? Who will it serve? How will it make their lives better? How long will people remember you and your life's work? It's been said that, as humans, we all have *two* death dates.

The first is the day we physically die, and the second is the day the last person who speaks our name dies. That's deep. Take a second to reread that sentence.

Our legacy continues after our physical death as long as people continue to remember our work and speak our name. Will your STUPID goal make such a long-lasting, positive impact that people will still be speaking your name one hundred years after you take your last breath? It absolutely can, and I believe it will!

5. **DREAM:** If something is in your head, it's a dream. If you write that dream on paper, it's a goal. If you verbalize that goal to the world, now it's a commitment. My challenge to you is to take your STUPID goal and write it down, then share it with the world. Sure, people will laugh at you. The masses laugh at every idea that doesn't fit inside society's normal, boring box. Now I want you to become obsessed with your STUPID goal. When you wake up in the morning, I want you to spend your first sixty seconds visualizing it as if you've already made it a reality. Before you go to bed at night, I want you to visualize it as if you've already made it a reality. During the day, I want you to speak your goal to the universe aloud—I do this in the shower each morning. As you do so, be sure to also affirm yourself regarding your goal. Positive self-talk will help build your confidence that you can make your goal a reality.

Your *obsessions will become your possessions* in life. Whatever you constantly think about and ask for will be what your brain searches for. The thoughts you have in your head will become what you have in your life. Dream big, allow these STUPID thoughts in your head, share your intentions with the world, and you'll live the life you desire.

CASTING A VISION

When you reflect on your school career, if you're anything like me, some of your favorite moments came during recreation time—arts and crafts, playing during recess, coloring, or any other activity that allowed you to get creative and be yourself.

It's time for you to tap into your creativity and even get a bit *crafty*. I want you to create a vision board. Pause here, close your eyes, and *picture, in great detail, what you believe to be your perfect future life*.

Welcome back! I specifically didn't give you detailed instructions for that exercise because I didn't want to steer your vision. After all, it's *your* vision, not mine. But I hope you didn't hold back—that you envisioned a life where your STUPID goals had become a reality.

Your vision may have been short-term or long-term in nature. It may have been things you can accomplish this year or things that could take a lifetime. Understand that your vision will change throughout your life. There will never be one final destination—though many people fail to realize this.

Too often people tell themselves things like, *Once I have this type of home, drive this type of car, have this much money in my bank account, then I will be fulfilled and happy.* Then they buy that house, drive that car, and have that money, only to discover they still aren't fulfilled and happy.

Maybe this kind of vision should come with a warning label that reads: "Acquiring all of these items is awesome, but they won't fulfill you on a deeper level." But another major reason that realizing this kind of vision feels hollow for some people is that their vision didn't evolve and expand as their journey through life did. Without realizing it, they were chasing after something they really didn't want anymore.

Again, I'm not saying to exclude materialistic things on your vision board—it's your vision, not mine. But I am reminding you that your vision today might not be the same as your vision a year from now, *and that's okay*. Once created, you will obsess over what you see on that board daily. You will keep it visible so you can visit it multiple times daily. And if there is ever a moment when something on that board no longer aligns with your values, beliefs, passion, or purpose, just update it!

Your vision needs to be adaptable to you. Consider taking the time to update your vision board at least once a year. Every once in a while, you may need to ask some key questions of yourself to see whether your vision for the future is still the direction in which you want to head. Here are a few key questions to get you started:

- Do my current goals reflect my core values and long-term aspirations?
- What has changed in my life since I last reviewed my vision?

- What successes have I experienced that indicate I'm moving in the right direction?
- Are there any recurring challenges or obstacles that suggest a misalignment or infeasibility with my vision?
- Do I feel motivated and excited about the goals I'm pursuing?
- Is there a sense of fulfillment and joy in the journey toward my vision?
- What new skills, knowledge, or experiences have I gained that contribute to my vision?
- Is there a healthy balance between striving for my vision and enjoying the present moment?
- Are there any new goals or desires that have emerged that should be integrated into my vision?
- What insights or lessons have I learned since my last review that could inform my current vision?

I want to challenge you to ask yourself the *why* behind the items you have chosen. There are surface wants, and then there are the reasons behind those wants. Oftentimes we stop at the surface rather than digging a little deeper to discover what we are truly looking for.

In addition to materialistic goals, you may realize you have desires for self-improvement. Are there books you want to read, skills you want to acquire, habits you want to build, or ideals you want to achieve? What about goals for your mental, emotional, physical, or spiritual health? Maybe you want to place a greater focus on relationships: your family, friends, mentors, and mentees. Or perhaps you're even thinking about your legacy already. What's the impact you hope to leave? All these are goals you may already hope for but haven't yet taken the time to think through. Before you get to making your vision board, take a moment to consider for yourself what goals align with where you are now.

For years my board was filled with materialistic visions. Today it still has a picture of the home on the lake that I will someday own. However, I've shifted from wanting to earn a million dollars each year to now wanting to donate a million dollars each year. In fact, writing this book has been on my board for years, and its resulting effect will help me take one step closer to my charitable goals as well. It takes time, but ultimately, everything you have on your vision board will begin to work together to help you realize your life's vision and purpose.

First, start by figuring out how you're going to put together your board. Everybody learns differently, has different styles, and processes information uniquely. Determine what works best for you. Do you like paper pictures? Do you prefer digital? Do you enjoy reading and writing written words? Or is it a combination of everything? There's no wrong answer here; pick the style you prefer.

Next, go back to your visions when I encouraged you to stop and picture your best life. What did you see? Take those images and make them real. Write them, print them, draw them, design them—whatever works for you.

And finally, create your board using those visions. Again, this could be on a poster or corkboard in your dorm or bedroom or as a wallpaper collage on your phone or laptop. It could be digital, handwritten, or a combination of all. Whatever works for you, make it happen.

In fact, do it now. Take a few moments to transfer your vision from your head to paper by writing down, in great detail, everything you see in your future. I'll wait.

Congratulations! You just took the first GIANT step toward making your vision a reality. You've heard me reference "the masses" and encourage you to take a "contrarian approach" to what the masses are doing. Well, by completing your vision board, you did just that! Nine out of ten humans on the planet have never moved the visions from their brains onto paper. You are now in an elite minority of people committed to making things happen.

Now for the hard part—*commiting to this exercise long-term*. Spend sixty seconds thinking about this vision as if it's already a reality each morning. Spend sixty more seconds thinking about this vision as if it's already a reality each evening. Physically look at this vision throughout the day, every day. Adjust your vision as your life evolves. Be patient. Everything worth having in this world is worth working for and waiting for. Everything you want is possible, but it won't happen overnight or without relentless focus.

THE JOURNEY TO FUTURE YOU

Perhaps the dumbest question you get in your teens is, "What are you going to do when you grow up?" Admittedly, I've fallen into this trap and have asked the same question of teens too. The question assumes there is a discernable answer, but there's not.

We can—and should—have dreams and visions for our lives, but it'd be foolish to think that our plans are set in stone. The reality is that nobody knows what's down the road. Far too many uncertainties and uncontrollable variables await each of us in the future. What happens if you get *this* job? Or make *that* connection? Don't get into *this* certain school? Or find out you actually love doing *that*?

Of course, you want to be setting STUPID Goals and casting a vision for your life to motivate and inspire you. But you don't want to hold that vision so tightly that it can't adjust as your values and desires do. Perhaps the better question than asking what you want to do when you grow up is, "What do you want to accomplish over the next *twelve months*?"

No one can predict life. If we are continually learning, improving, and evolving, our journeys may take us to places that we may not have previously known about, that we never considered an option, or that hadn't existed before.

By the time I turned thirty, I had worked seven different jobs and lived in nine different apartments, condos, and homes. I had made money and lost money. I had done work that excited me as well as work I wouldn't wish upon my greatest enemy. Through this journey of changes, successes, and defeats, I learned a little something about myself at each crossroad. I didn't realize it at the time, but I was assembling a version of Future Me—the person I would ultimately become. Bit by bit, each crossroad helped to form me into the person I am today.

When I was leaving my teenage years, I allowed my work to define my success. I was chasing a unicorn—which is to say, something that didn't exist. I didn't yet realize that every time you scale a mountain, you see a bigger, unconquered one yet ahead. Defining success by achievement never actually produces contentment. So you can't define your success by your own achievement, or you'll never really be satisfied.

Everything in life changes when you realize true success is found in making the most of your journey. So many of your experiences in life will be more about *the kind of person they are molding you into* than about the work itself. And those character-forming experiences are golden. The satisfaction from being a person you can be proud of will far outstrip anything you can get from any one achievement.

Throughout life, you'll likely have any number of jobs, relationships, and other venture that don't seem to work out. If you define success by achievement, those letdowns may be crushing. However, when you look at those experiences through the lens of character formation, you see that they're accomplishing just what you need. With each one, you live a little more and learn a little more. You get to know what you want and who you are. You build your wisdom, resilience, and sense of self. In the moment, I didn't always love the seemingly dead-end jobs or relational breakups, but looking back, I wouldn't have it any other way. Those experiences made me who I am.

So spend less time stressing about what you want to do and more time on who you want to be. What does that best version of you look like? Don't stress that you're not there yet. Appreciate where you are now, but don't trick yourself into thinking this is all you can be. That way, you can move with confidence toward becoming the Future You that you want to be.

Now that you've given yourself an incredible vision of your future, it's time to take a hard look at the roadblocks that may keep you from making this vision a reality.

CHAPTER TWO

WARNING: SELF-IMPOSED LIMITS

*If you live for people's acceptance,
you'll die from their rejection.*

—LECRAE

I fundamentally knew everything I needed to know about being a happy, healthy, successful human by the time I finished the fifth grade. I then spent the next thirty years listening to a voice that was trying to prove me wrong. As with most people, that inner voice held me back for many years—that is, until I learned how to silence it.

Let's turn back the clock. We'll start in kindergarten. Kindergarten was a lot of fun. Teachers read to us. We colored. We did crafts. There was playtime, snack time, and even nap time. Kindergarten was fun.

Then came first grade. In the first grade, I had friends: Pat, Joe, Chris, Kristy, Heather—all people I had met in kindergarten. We played a little bit over the summer, and coming back to first grade, there they were again—my friends.

I got to second grade, and I learned about fitness. I started playing sports like soccer, basketball, and baseball. I learned how to compete with others. I was having fun, I was with my friends, and I was staying fit and active. Life was good.

When I got to third grade, I realized none of this was possible without my family. I didn't have a job, money, or a car. What I did have was a lot of questions that I didn't know the answers to. But my family had all those things! They were able to help me in the areas that I needed. So I learned the value of family.

Moving down the line, we get to fourth grade. And in fourth grade, my friends picked up on the fact that I was pretty good at school. I was pretty much a straight-A student, so my friends thought it would be funny to give me the nickname Bookworm. They liked it. *I didn't*. But they were relentless about it.

Finally, I said, "Guys, I don't like that nickname. It kind of hurts my feelings."

And so they apologized. And what did I do? I forgave them. So in fourth grade, I learned the power of forgiveness.

Then I got to fifth grade, and for the first time in my life, *I failed*. It didn't make sense. I thought I was pretty smart! It happened with a science test. I didn't really like science. (I still don't.) My teacher handed me the graded exam. It read: "60%." As I stared down at that paper—that bright-red "60%"—I got butterflies in my stomach and a lump in my throat. I was fighting back tears. And for the first time in my life, I heard the voice:

Scott.

Yeah?

You are a failure.

I am?

Yes. You failed. Smart people don't fail tests. You did. You are a failure.

Hmm. I guess I am.

In her book, *Worthy*, Jamie Kern Lima challenges readers to reflect on the first time they they knew the answer to a question in class but didn't raise their hand. For me, that was the day after I failed the science test.

My teacher asked a question. I knew the answer, but instead of raising my hand, I kept my hand by my side. I stayed silent. I listened to that voice saying, *Don't do it. Don't raise your hand. You'll get it wrong. Everyone will laugh at you. It'll be so embarrassing.* And so I sat in silence. I let the teacher call on a classmate who gave the same answer I was going to give. She got it right. I would have gotten it right.

I knew the answer to that question. In fact, I fundamentally knew everything I needed to know to be a happy, healthy, successful human by the time I finished fifth grade. Have fun, hang with friends, stay fit and active, love your family, and be forgiving. But when I got to failure, instead of looking at the 40 percent I got wrong and using it as feedback to figure out what went wrong, I allowed my failure to define me. And I allowed that to keep happening for the better part of the next thirty years of my life.

I'm going to ask a girl to a dance! *Don't do it. She'll say no.*

I'll apply to a good college! *Don't bother. You'll get rejected.*

I should send my résumé to a better-paying job. *Don't waste your time. They'll pick someone else.*

I let it happen time and time again. I allowed that voice to hold me back.

Studies show that the average elementary student will laugh up to three hundred times a day. The average adult will laugh about fifteen. The louder that voice gets, the less happy and less successful we are, and the more limited our potential becomes. But here's the deal: we all have that voice.

I thought it was just me. But then I heard Tony Robbins speak about how we're all born with a primitive brain. We have outdated equipment in all of our skulls. Our brains have two primary functions: to keep us running efficiently and to keep us safe. The best way that our brains know to keep us safe is by talking us out of taking chances, taking risks, and leaving our comfort zone.

But here's the problem. When you don't take chances, when you don't take risks, and when you don't leave your comfort zone, you never get to experience all the amazing opportunities that life has to offer. You never give yourself the chance to become the happiest, healthiest, most successful version of you that you're destined to be.

So that voice is in all of us. And it's never going away. But we know that it's robbing us of our unlimited potential. What do we do about it? Well, in our current digital age, we go to one of our apps. Or alternatively, we go to our APS. We *Acknowledge* the voice, we *Prove* it wrong, and then we *Silence* it.

And the way that works is pretty simple. Start by acknowledging the voice:

"I hear you, voice. I know you're just trying to do your job and keep me safe."

Then you prove it wrong:

"I have had success in the past. Things have worked out for me. I have won competitions."

And finally, you silence it:

"I got this. Now, shhhhh . . ."

You take that chance, you don't hold yourself back, and you move forward into the unknown.

What you just read was an excerpt from a TEDx talk I gave. Here is the link to that talk: Learning to Silence Self-Doubt. When I was a teenager, other than snakes, public speaking was the scariest thing on the planet to me. But thirty years later, I did what I never believed I could and shared my message with the world. Before walking onstage, I acknowledged my inner critic's voice, proved it wrong, and silenced it. I didn't let my inner critic win—and neither should you.

THE FIGHT AGAINST SIN

The road to your next adventure is riddled with obstacles. Some of these will be outside your control, but many will come from within. In this chapter, I'll walk you through some of the most common self-imposed limits that can keep you from chasing after your STUPID goals, and I'll equip you with the tools you'll need to handle each obstacle as it comes.

As I've said, taking on a contrarian viewpoint is vital for you to achieve exceptional results. If you want to be successful—to stand out—you have to be willing to think differently. The difficulty is that people don't usually like it when you do. Whenever you fail to conform to "the masses," you'll likely be questioned or judged. As the Japanese proverb says, "The nail that sticks out gets hammered down."

It can be hard to stand alone. Your confidence can become so tied up with the voices of others when they start to get in your head. You begin to question yourself. Then, whenever you don't see immediate results, it feels like mounting evidence that the voices were right all along.

These feelings are what I call the pathway to SIN—but probably not the kind of sin you're thinking about. I'm not talking about the moral shortcomings they tell you about in Sunday school. No, this kind of SIN comes in the forms of *Self-doubt*, *Inner criticism*, and *Negative self-talk*.

Many young adults (all adults actually) grapple with self-doubt, especially when facing new experiences, like starting a new school, learning a new subject, applying for jobs, or exploring one's passions. This can be especially challenging when you don't realize that it's actually a common feeling. Impostor syndrome kicks in, and you start to believe the lie that you don't have what it takes to be where you are.

The inner critic can be particularly harsh during the formative years. Social media amplifies feelings of inadequacy. And when you fail to challenge the negative voices in your head, your natural instinct is to ignore the 99 percent good to focus on the 1 percent bad.

That all contributes to your personal narrative—the story you tell yourself about yourself—which can be easily colored by negative self-talk. You see it all the time. It's when you think, *I'm not the kind of person who can achieve an unbelievable dream*; *I'm not worthy of being introduced to other people's networks;* or *I don't have any qualities that make me stand out.* And without the skills to reframe negative self-talk into positive affirmations, this kind of personal narrative can significantly impact your self-esteem and overall mental health.

Sadly, most people don't know how to respond when SIN creeps into their minds. The little voices of doubt become louder and louder, and the feeling of defeat becomes stronger and stronger. Eventually, you buy that false bill of goods. You give up. Let me challenge you to consider a better response: replace *quit* with *grit*.

But how do you do that? How do you keep doing all the things you know you need to do, even when you don't see the results and feel like you want to quit? Here's the key: *the people who learn to control their minds will control their results*. It's a game of mental warfare—with battles being fought daily.

As writer Robin Sharma explains, "What you focus on grows, what you think about expands, and what you dwell upon determines your destiny." This means that if you focus on self-doubt, inner criticism, and negative self-talk, you'll naturally start to see more and more examples of failure to confirm the narrative you're already telling yourself.

But the inverse is also true. If you remind yourself that you're playing the long game, planting seeds, and rolling that little snowball down the hill to gain momentum and reap the benefits later, it will serve as a helpful reminder that you are on the right track. In the game of mental warfare, this is how you perform a tactical counterstrike.

There are a number of ways to practically shift your mindset and give yourself these vital reminders. First, you can counter negative self-talk with positive affirmations. Start each day with a list of positive affirmations about yourself that remind you why you are capable and worthy.

Second, consider starting a gratitude journal. Writing down things you are grateful for can shift your focus from negative thoughts to the positive aspects of your life.

Third, scrutinize your negative thoughts. It's a good practice to seriously question the validity of your negative self-talk. Is what you are telling yourself based more in reality or just your fears?

Finally, surround yourself with voices of positivity. Spend time with people in your support system who uplift and support you more than they tear you down.

Even still, you will be regularly flooded with unavoidable naysayers who will tempt you to give up and give in. When you're not sure you have what it takes to be exceptional, it's not hard to find reasons to skip the work, to let others do your thinking for you, and to become "copy-and-paste." All around you are people and programs offering shortcuts to success. Nobody will blame you for conforming to the norm.

Fighting through obstacles with the grit needed to accomplish your goals is hard. But so too is not meeting the STUPID goals you've set for yourself. Settling for a life of mediocrity and a professional career that gets overshadowed by those willing to do the work will leave you unsatisfied and unfulfilled. Living a life of regret may be the hardest thing you can do. *You have to choose your hard.*

So if either path is hard, which challenging path should you choose to navigate each day? The one that delays present gratification for long-term fulfillment? Or the one that gives instant ease but will inevitably leave you disappointed after all is said and done? If you're looking for a happiness that will last, you have to refuse to settle for ease.

Fighting the mental warfare game requires faith. In my view, faith is simply *a person's ability to see invisible results.* When you are doing all the things that you know will eventually get you to the places you want to be but aren't seeing results, it can be hard. Your grit propels you to walk down that hard path, but you also need faith to visualize the end goal and see it through.

Those who play the mental warfare game at the highest levels know it's all about the *start* and the *finish.* Starting something new can be daunting and downright scary. It requires change, which is one of the things that scares humans most.

But even for those who do take the leap of faith to start something new, the voices of SIN so often lead them to quit on their grit and bail on their faith. What these people don't realize is that they are only *extending* the hard path by jumping back to the starting line of something else. But that path will inevitably lead to obstacles too. What will happen to those people then?

Don't let your response be to quit. Fight and win the mental warfare game. Have the courage to *start*, the *grit* to work your plan daily, and the *faith* to keep going even when everyone and everything around you says you should quit.

THE FEAR OF REJECTION

Most of our self-imposed limits are rooted in some kind of fear. Fear is something that's deeply seated in all of us, and many of our fears can be traced back to one deep-rooted anchor fear that acts as the built-in, standard operating equipment in all of us from the time of birth: *our fear of rejection.*

Everyone wants to be part of the in-group, to have people like them. We crave acceptance from others. When people criticize us, we get upset. We don't want to be left alone or left out. And unless you're a narcissist, you've probably doubted at some point whether you'll be included or wanted somewhere.

Rejection validates those lies we tell ourselves. For instance, if you didn't think you were confident or prepared to take on a challenging task but still tried it and failed, that rejection might serve as a reminder that you were right about yourself all along. You asked the question or took the risk, only to be told no. In your mind, you lost.

So how do you overcome your inherent fear of rejection? *You get used to being rejected.* Think of rejection as a muscle you can train to get stronger. An athlete lifts weights to strengthen muscles. In the beginning, they may be able to bench press 100 pounds five times. However, after months of training, they can bench press 100 pounds twelve times and do it easily.

You can lessen your fear of rejection by doing the same. The more you train yourself to face it, the stronger you get, and the less fear lives inside you. Psychology tells us this works, and therapists use this kind of technique all the time to help people face their fears through exposure therapy. If you challenge yourself to do just *one thing* each day that scares you and that will likely lead to rejection, it will become less scary. Then do two each day. Then do three. Suddenly, after a few months, your fear of rejection is nearly gone. Now you have more confidence and are more likely to take on meaningful work. The more you hear the word *no*, the less it scares you, and the less the fear of rejection has control over you.

Ironically, we spend so many of our younger years fearing rejection and being told no that we stop pursuing the things we desire the most. Then, when we get to the years at the end of our lives and look back, we realize the biggest regrets are from not pursuing more of the things we desired the most.

Dr. Kevin Elko, a sports psychologist and career-enhancement consultant, shared two simple questions at a seminar I attended years ago that changed my life forever. He told us to ask ourselves: *So what?* and *Now what?*

After any rejection or *no* in your life, ask yourself these two magical questions. Asking yourself, "So what?" helps to minimize the emotional impact of rejection. It encourages you to step back and see the rejection as just one event in the broader scope of your life. This one setback doesn't define you or your future. Failure is not the end; it's feedback—and just one part of the journey.

Asking yourself, "Now what?" shifts your focus from the past rejection to your next steps. It encourages proactive thinking and planning. What are the constructive actions you can take next? Instead of dwelling on the rejection, how can you seek to find solutions and alternative paths?

Fixating on the past rejection will only get you stuck in a place of self-defeat. And fixating on the future fallout of having been rejected will lead you to a place of endless anxiety. But by asking yourself these two simple questions, you remind yourself of an important truth: you have very little control over the *external events* that happen to you in your life. You can't control everything, and trying to do so will only lead to frustration and anger. What you can control—the only thing you can really control—is your *response* to the events that happen to you.

Write down this formula: *Event + Response = Outcome* (E + R = O). We just covered the event (E). Again, you have almost no control over the events that happen to you in your life. The one thing you can control is your response (R) to each event. And it's your response that determines the ultimate outcome (O).

Create a three-second pause between an event and your response to that event. Saying nothing is always smarter than saying the wrong thing. People can't hear your thoughts, and taking three seconds to think allows deeper consideration to your words before you speak them.

In those three seconds, take a moment to do a few things. First, acknowledge the rejection. Feel its sting. It's natural to feel disappointed, but limit this feeling to just a moment.

"I've been rejected. This hurts, but it doesn't define me."

Next, mentally ask yourself, "So what?" Put things in perspective. "So what if they didn't accept me? This one event doesn't determine my worth or my future. Many successful people have faced rejection and still achieved great things."

Finally, ask yourself, "Now what?" The only thing you can totally control is your response. Is the next step to apply to another college, to seek feedback, to improve your skills, or to explore some other opportunities? Think to yourself, "Now what can I do to move forward? What are my next steps? How can I use this rejection to fuel my growth and resilience?"

By asking these questions, you take control of your narrative. You're not letting rejection define you. Instead, you're using it as a stepping stone. Reframing the situation turns the negative experience into a learning opportunity. It builds your mental resilience so you can better face future rejection while also enabling you to get back up with actionable steps in response to the setback of being told no.

Unfortunately, bad things happen to good people every day. You will be rejected. You will be told no. You will meet ignorant people who say ignorant things. You will work your tail off and still be told it wasn't enough. You must understand that you can't always avoid these events. They're outside your sphere of control. *They aren't your fault.* What you *can* control is your response, and that's what you're responsible for. Don't rush it. Respond wisely. The outcome of your life depends on it.

THE FEAR OF FAILURE

Similar to the fear of rejection is the fear of failure. However, while the fear of rejection focuses on the response and judgment of others, the fear of failure is centered on personal performance and desired outcomes. It's *internally* driven by self-criticism and high standards, whereas the fear of rejection is *externally* driven by the opinions and acceptance of others.

The fear of failure is the apprehension you feel that you will not succeed in achieving your goals. This fear can paralyze you, preventing you from even trying due to the potential for embarrassment, disappointment, or loss. The fear of failure often stems from a perfectionist mindset, where anything less than success is seen as a personal flaw.

Do you ever sit out of a group game because you don't think you'll be any good at it? Or avoid playing a sport because you anticipate losing? Do you stay on the sidelines instead of getting on the dance floor because you don't think you'd be as good at it as you'd like to be? Whatever the case, if you've ever kept yourself from trying something because you determine it's not worth doing unless you know that you'll be able to get it just right, you know exactly what I'm talking about.

How do you avoid this kind of paralysis? First, as with the fear of rejection, you have to be able to reframe your fear. In this case, redefine for yourself what it means to fail. Failure is a part of the learning process. Every successful person has failed hundreds of times. But to be successful, they didn't let failing stop them. Instead, they viewed their failures as opportunities to learn and grow. The key is to *fail forward*. Embrace each failure as a stepping stone to success.

That requires getting a little more comfortable with messing up. Overcoming the fear of failure doesn't happen when you stop failing. It happens when you change the way you think about it. When you see it simply as a stepping stone to success, you're set free to laugh at yourself a little more and try things that you don't anticipate being perfect at.

Second, set realistic goals. Now, that's not to say that you shouldn't be pursuing your unrealistic, STUPID Goals—not at all. I want you to chase after those incredible dreams. But the best way to do so is to break down your big goals into smaller, more manageable tasks. Jot down one or two essential tasks that you can focus on for *only* the day ahead. Make your aim each morning be to "win the day." This makes your big goals less intimidating and allows you to celebrate the small, daily victories. Then, as you accomplish these daily goals, focus on building win streaks to create momentum and raise your confidence level. Even if you have a day or two that don't go quite as you'd have liked, your momentum will keep these road bumps from stopping you in your tracks.

Finally, see the connection between your fear of failure and SIN (those pesky feelings of self-doubt, inner criticism, and negative self-talk). A big part of grappling with the fear of failure is replacing negative self-talk with positive affirmations. Oftentimes people talk to themselves in degrading ways that they would never tolerate if it were coming from anyone else. Don't treat yourself that way! Encourage yourself as you would a friend.

Instead of saying, "I'll never be able to do this," tell yourself, "I can learn from this and get better." Our inner critic is incredibly quick when it comes to jumping in and forming our instinctive reactions. But the more you intentionally counter this voice, the quieter your inner critic will become. Eventually, you may get to the place where your instinct becomes positive self-talk as your confidence grows.

Failing can be scary. Too often we tie our value as a person to our successfulness. Then we hold ourselves back from trying at all for fear of what a potential failure may say about our worth. We forget that the greatest possible failure is the failure to try and that learning how to fall down is actually what it takes to become the kind of person who always gets back up.

THE FEAR OF SUCCESS

Maybe your problem isn't questioning whether you're enough or whether you'll be able to meet your own standards. It could be that the future responsibilities, pressures, and changes that will inevitably come with achieving your goals drive you to fear succeeding altogether.

The fear of success is the anxiety that comes with achieving your goals. It may sound counterintuitive, but succeeding can introduce many new factors to life that some find daunting.

You might be worried that you won't be able to maintain your success if you finally reach your goal. Nobody wants to be a one-hit-wonder turned has-been. What happens if you peak too young and then the rest of your life is spent trying to relive the glory days?

More likely, you may think that if you succeed, you'll face higher expectations. Your boss, teacher, or parents will ask more and more from you, and you don't think you are prepared to deal with that. If you don't keep up the high level of performance, you fear that you'll inevitably become a disappointment to others.

Perhaps you anxiously anticipate dealing with envy or resentment from other people. Once you become the boss, people treat you differently. You no longer get to be buddy-buddy around the water cooler. And people will try to knock you down a peg when you're the king of the hill, right? You can't stay on top forever.

Let me give you a few tips for how to counter this fear of success. First, visualize positive outcomes. Focus on the benefits of success and how it will positively impact your life and the lives of those around you. Will the success you're hoping for give you new, life-giving connections? Will it provide you with the freedom from debt you've been looking for? Will it develop you into a better person or enable you to help others?

If you take the time to objectively conduct a cost-benefit analysis, odds are you'll see that accomplishing your goal will produce a net positive result. If that's the case, don't let the potential negatives carry more weight than is due them. Just like when you created a vision board for your goals, use visualization techniques to imagine your life with your goal achieved, and remind yourself of the positive aspects of success.

Second, you'll need to prepare yourself for change. Understand that success will bring changes but that change is a natural part of growth. Embrace it as a positive force. Your success may indeed come with new responsibilities and expectations, but that shouldn't hold you back. Create a plan for how you want to handle these new responsibilities and expectations that come with success so you aren't caught off guard.

Third, just like dealing with the fear of failure, overcoming your fear of success is benefited by taking small, gradual steps. Anticipating all the change that may come from success can be overwhelming, but if you're taking bit-sized steps to achieve that success, you'll be able to adjust to the changes as they come. What's more, it will give you the confidence to see that the success that you feared maintaining successfully is actually something sustainable.

Finally, stay grounded. Keep a balanced perspective, and remember why you started your journey in the first place. Success should not change who you are at your core. Regularly remind yourself of your values and the reasons behind your goals, and you'll be able to keep who you are regardless of the evolving world around you.

Regardless of the fear you may face—whether it be rejection, failure, or success—the road to overcoming self-imposed limits is paved with developed resilience, systems of support, and continual adjustment. Cultivate a growth mindset where unexpected challenges are seen as opportunities to grow. Surround yourself with positive influences who encourage and support your goals.

And whenever you experience rejection, failure, or success, take time to reflect on what you've learned, and identify how you can improve. You won't regret it.

REGRETS NONETHELESS

I'm sure by now you've already done a few things in your life that you regret. I'm also sure there have been a few things you regret not doing. Spoiler alert—you will have plenty more regrets of both kinds for the rest of your life.

People will tell you that they have *no regrets*. Personally, I think that's a lie. And to take it a step further, I wouldn't even say that'd be something to brag about. Regrets aren't a bad thing to have. At their core, *regrets are simply recognition*. In every instance, you either recognize you did something right, did something wrong, or missed an opportunity to do something altogether. None of that is bad. It would be far worse to lack the self-awareness to recognize one of those things had happened.

Regret is a common emotion that everyone experiences at some point in their lives. It's okay to feel regret as long as you know how to respond to it. Acknowledge your emotions and understand why you feel this way. Oftentimes regret stems from missed opportunities, poor decisions, or actions we wish we hadn't taken. While regrets can be painful, they also offer valuable lessons if we choose to learn from them rather than dwell on them.

To learn from regret, reflect on what you could have done differently and how you can apply these lessons in the future. Keeping a journal is one way to do this that may be helpful for you to look back on when planning for future decisions.

Use your regret as a catalyst for positive change. Regret forces you to reflect on your actions, which can lead to personal growth and better future choices. The discomfort of regret can motivate you to take action and make changes to avoid feeling the same way again. If you regret not taking a chance on something, make a commitment to seize similar opportunities in the future. Whether it's applying for a challenging job, traveling, or learning a new skill, take proactive steps to avoid future regrets.

It's also important to forgive yourself. Understand that everyone makes mistakes. *It's a part of being human.* Be kind to yourself and let go of the past. Holding on to past mistakes only hinders your progress.

Instead of dwelling on the past, focus on the present. Focus on what you can control now. Again, it's all about your *response*. The past cannot be changed, but you do have the power to shape your future.

The secret sauce to ensure a positive response is remembering to *call an internal timeout*. Taking a pause isn't just a tool to help you bounce back after experiencing rejection; pausing can also help you avoid making regretful, rash decisions. Don't rush your decision-making or blurt out the first thing that enters your head. Instead, call an internal timeout and ask yourself, "Is this something I will regret doing or not doing?" The more decisions you make following those brief time-outs, the fewer regrets you'll have.

In college I had the opportunity to join a student exchange program that would allow me to spend a semester studying abroad. I hesitated, worrying about missing out on my social life and falling behind in my studies. Ultimately, I decided not to apply. Now, over twenty years later, my friends who participated in the program still speak passionately about the incredible experiences and lifelong friendships they made. Hearing their stories makes me regret my choice. I realize I had missed a unique opportunity to grow and learn. I won't make that kind of mistake again.

Many of our regrets come from letting opportunities pass us by. I know this because some of the top reported regrets by dying people include wishing that they had taken more risks, had lived their dream, had done more for others, or had chosen more meaningful work. What's missing from that list? None of them listed wishing they had avoided fear, failure, or rejection. None wished they had taken fewer risks, passed on more adventures, or pursued smaller goals.

Throughout your life, you will face decisions that offer two basic choices: You can either (1) take the path of least resistance and do what's easy or (2) take the road less traveled and do what scares you. I'm here to remind you that the easy option will always be available. That's what makes it easy. But I'm also here to challenge you to fast-forward to your ninetieth birthday and ask yourself, "Would that version of me be proud of or regret this decision?" That answer will often provide your best decision at such a crossroad.

One of the greatest self-improvement routines you can have is spending regular time with the elderly. They've *been there* and *done that*. They know what worked and what didn't. And trust me, they don't hold back when it comes to the things they are proud of and the things they regret. Seriously, just ask them. Their perspective may be what it takes to give you the courage to tackle and overcome your fears of rejection, failure, or success.

You'll always have regrets. Even if you are self-aware and remember to call those internal timeouts, you'll still think or tell yourself you could have done more. Or you'll wish you could take something back. *It's natural.* But regrets don't have to be a negative force. By acknowledging your regrets, learning from them, and taking positive action, you can turn your "what-ifs" into "what's next?" Remember, every experience—good or bad—contributes to your growth and helps to shape Future You.

CHAPTER THREE

BETTER THOUGHTS BEYOND THIS POINT

A positive attitude may not solve all your problems, but it will annoy enough people to make it worth the effort.

—HERM ALBRIGHT

By this point, you may have realized just how much of your success on this journey hinges on your mindset. Whether you're adopting a contrarian perspective, setting goals, and casting a vision—or you're overcoming the inner voice of SIN, working through your fears, and learning from your regrets—it all boils down to having the right mindset.

In this chapter, I'm going to share a few more key mindsets and thought patterns that I've come to recognize as critical for making your way toward a successful career and life. If you've made it this far in the book, it tells me two things about you:

1. You are serious about learning and improving day by day; and
2. You truly love and care about the version of you that awaits this world in the future.

It takes a long time to get to Future You. It takes patience to get to the place where you are living the truly rich and significant life you deserve.

ATTITUDE, ACTIONS, AND EFFORT

Do you want to be losing by two touchdowns after the first quarter? Of course not. Yet even when the scoreboard clearly indicates you're behind, that certainly doesn't mean you've lost yet. Plenty of time remains. Games aren't won in the first quarter.

Life is no different, except your quarters are longer, which just allows you more time to adjust, recover from failures, and create momentum toward a comeback. So be patient. All good things will eventually come to those who wait.

Understand that oftentimes in life, your wins will be a result of your losses. Winning is easy. If all you ever did in life was succeed at your first attempt, what fun would that be? On the surface, you would think it'd be great. But the only way to consistently succeed at everything you do is to not only do the things you are already good at. You can master something insignificant that doesn't fulfill you and succeed every time. However, that complacent path only leads to emptiness. You'll live a boring life where you don't ask people for things you want, you don't try new things that you may love, and when challenges present themselves, rather than risking failure, you just quit.

During your younger days, you'll succeed at avoiding temporary pain, but by taking this approach, you'll have cheated Future You out of long-term happiness. Don't be afraid to take some chances in life. Trying and failing takes patience, but you'll learn something from every challenge you pursue.

The easiest way in the world to make yourself miserable is to focus solely on your results. If you only judge yourself based on your outcomes, you'll be miserable for 70 percent of your life. Why is that? Simply put, if you truly seek to become the most amazing version of Future You, you will lose more often than you win. As a rule of thumb, people who push out of their comfort zones and try something new will fail 70 percent of the time. So if you only focus on results, that's how much you'll be disappointed.

But what if you focused on the only things you *can* control: your attitude, actions, and effort? What if you went into all ten of those challenges with a positive attitude, took massive action, and gave 100 percent of your focused effort? Regardless of the result, you'd be happy because you tried your best and gave it your all. Ten out of ten times, this will lead you to happiness. Three out of those ten, it will even lead you to *elation* because, on top of your attitude, actions, and effort, you found success too.

Understand that Future You will not be determined by the results of your life but by your laserlike focus on how you approach your attitude, actions, and effort. Those are the things that forge the kind of person you are becoming. Remain focused in those three areas, and the results will take care of themselves.

Billionaire businessman Mark Cuban once said that it only takes one great idea to change your life forever. The most famous example of this is Thomas Edison. You know him as the man who invented the lightbulb. However, you may not know him as the man who failed to invent the lightbulb over ten thousand times!

During his childhood, one of Edison's teachers told him he was "too stupid to learn anything." Edison was fired from his first job because his work did not produce results. During one of his failed experiments with the lightbulb, Edison burned down his laboratory! Through it all, Edison focused on the things he could control: his attitude, actions, and effort. When asked by a reporter how he could persevere through ten thousand failures, Edison famously responded, "I have not failed. I just found ten thousand ways that won't work." If you want to experience a happy, fulfilled life, fall in love with the process of *trying*.

Edison understood that he had to fight through setbacks to accomplish something that would make Future Edison proud—along with the rest of the world. He died in 1931, nearly one hundred years ago, yet we still tell stories about him and enjoy the product he worked tirelessly to create. Control only the things you can control, don't focus on results, and understand it only takes one big idea to succeed. Regardless of the outcome, this approach will lead you to the best possible version of Future You.

PROCRASTINATORS' MEETING RESCHEDULED FOR LATER

One of the major forces that drove me to write this book was my years spent working with adults who are desperately trying to improve. I asked myself whether these amazing people—who are essentially just struggling with the basics—would be in their situation today if they knew in their teens the mindsets that would be essential for their journey. How much different would their adult lives be if they had started forming the right habits and mental pathways when they were younger?

Of all the self-improvement lessons people would benefit from learning in their teens, the one most adults need help with is *time management*. When it comes to time management, there is one word that will derail your time efficiency and add stress and anxiety to your life without you even realizing it. That word is *later*.

Yup, I want you to become a hater of the word *later*. Why? Because if quitting is the easiest thing in the world to do, waiting until later is the second easiest. I've seen countless people live what I refer to as a "later life."

I'm going to start eating healthily . . . *next week*. I'm going to start exercising . . . *on Monday*. I'm going to go back to college . . . *next semester*. I'm going to take that vacation . . . *next year*. I'm going to tell that person how I really feel . . . *as soon as I get the courage*. I'm going to buy that house . . . *as soon as I have more money*. I'm going to volunteer at a nonprofit . . . *as soon as I have more time*. I'm going to spend more time with my family . . . *as soon as I get all my work done*.

Do you see how we trick ourselves as humans? Never once during those "I'm going to" statements did you ever read the word "later," but it was there. What might not be there is actually following up when "later" does come.

You see, that's the funny thing about "later." Some people get theirs, and some people don't. The Dave Matthews Band has a song called "Cry Freedom," which says, "The future is no place to place your better days." You don't always get the "later" that you were hoping for. Oftentimes the "I'll do it later" approach lasts for thirty-plus years, and then that person is gone, or their health is gone, or their money is gone, or the opportunity or person they were waiting for is gone.

Remember this maxim: "The past is gone, and the future may never come, so the present is all we get. That's why the *present* is a *gift*." Don't throw away your gift by waiting to open it in the future. You would never wait a week, month, or year to open a Christmas or birthday gift you were given, so don't do that with your time! Always remember the greatest gift is the one received each morning: a new day filled with countless opportunities. Don't wait—open that gift now and enjoy your present. Don't allow "later" to steal any of your days.

You won't always feel ready, and you'll often be tempted to wait until later. But the thing is, you'll never be 100 percent ready to do anything you desire, so choose to take imperfect action. An imperfect action is always better than having a perfect plan that you'll never execute. It's okay to try and fail. Failure is where most processes start, remember? Your goal is just that: *to start*.

Ditch "later." Identify what's most important to you today. Close your eyes, hold your breath, and jump into it. Sometimes it will be scary, but I promise you'll figure it out. And after every jump, you'll look back with delight because you dared to make the leap into the life you deserve.

DITCH "BUT" TO KICK BUTT

Let's talk about a second word that will slow you down on your journey to the best version of Future You. We'll talk in the car. I'll drive.

We're on the highway now, traveling at about seventy miles an hour. I ask why you decided not to attend that college that you really wanted to attend.

You say, "Well, I was going to go there, but—"

Suddenly, I slam on the brakes, and our speed drops to forty miles an hour. The person driving behind us slams on their brakes, honks the horn, and curses as they speed by. I accelerate again, and cars fly past us as I work back up to driving seventy.

"Sorry about that," I say. "Let's talk about something else. Tell me about that job you applied to. It seemed to be something you'd enjoy, and the pay was reasonable."

You tell me, "Yeah, it may have been a good opportunity, but—"

The car abruptly stops again, so quickly that you have to put your hands on the dash to prevent your head from flying through the windshield. Once again, horns are blasting, people are yelling, and every other vehicle on the highway speeds on by as we try to figure out what's happening with our car.

We accelerate back up to seventy miles an hour. I try to lighten the mood. "Gosh, I can't believe that happened again. How about we talk about something lighter? Music! You love to write lyrics for music. How has that been going?"

You begin to tell me, "I do love to write lyrics. It's something I was consistently doing for a while, but—"

There's a screeeeeeeching of tires, horns are blaring, and cars fly by. You and I sit on the side of the highway, stunned.

What in the world is going on?

One of my many wishes for you is to kick butt in life. However, to do so, the first thing you need to do is kick the "but" out of your life. Typically, everything that follows the word "but" is an excuse on some level—oftentimes an excuse to push something to *later.*

Try asking someone close to you why they've kicked something important to them down the road. Odds are their response will start with a confirmation that *yes, they wanted to do the thing*—and inevitably finish with an excuse following the word "but."

At this point in your journey, you are loaded with talent and potential, and your car travels fast on the highway toward Future You. Every time you wait until later or justify not doing something important to you using the word "but," your car slows down. While your brakes are burning, those who aren't waiting until "later" and have already eliminated "but" from their vocabulary fly by you.

When it comes to real-life driving, of course, you want to be safe and maintain a realistic speed. But when it comes to figurative driving on your life's highway, put the pedal to the metal and let it fly! Every car you pass has chosen to wait for something else or has believed the words that came after "but."

The greatest possession you'll ever own in life is your time. Time doesn't care if you feel ready, lack confidence, or are scared. Time has no interest in your opportunities, bank account, or relationships. Time waits for no one. It just keeps going whether you are ready or not—with or without you. Tomorrow you will wake up one day older and one day closer to the end of the time you get. When you stand at the crossroad of doing it now or waiting, I'd recommend you just do it now.

As humans, we never think we have enough time in our days. We also believe our lives will never end. Both statements are inaccurate. Every day has plenty of time, so long as you only focus on the few essential items. Even if you had more time, you'd find more ways to fill it and still feel like you don't have enough of it. At the same time, all lives will end, so waiting until later to do whatever it is you most desire is a long-term recipe for failure or disappointment.

With every challenge we face, we have only two choices: make it happen or make excuses. The excuses often arrive after the word "but," so stop your sentences before you get there. Own whatever words you just said—good or bad—and adjust as you move forward. Be where your feet are. Fully immerse yourself in the present. Whatever you are doing, do it. There are no "buts" about it.

GIVERS AND TAKERS

It's all too easy to adopt the majority mindset—whether that's focusing on results, pushing things till later, or letting "but" hold you back. But one of the most common mindset traps that I see today is the tendency for people to become "takers."

The good news is that you don't have to fall into this trap. You've learned the contrarian way, remember? Simply put, when masses of people are all running one way, the contrarian runs in the other direction. When a large group is all thinking and acting the same, the contrarian explores opposite points of view and actions. So let's take a look at the scarcity mindset from the contrarian perspective.

From a very young age, you were conditioned to take. You took food, the clothes you were given, and the home you lived in. You often wanted to take additional things you saw, like candy at the store, another ride on the merry-go-round, or a specific toy. More often than not, you got what you wanted—though sometimes it might have required a temper tantrum to get it.

Like it or not, you were programmed to believe that taking was a good thing. This programming might have led you to a path of entitlement. Entitlement is when you feel like you deserve to be given things, even when you technically haven't earned them. This is a dangerous path that many adults never leave.

My challenge to you is to begin the process of rewiring your taker mentality. It won't be easy, but it will be necessary to create true happiness in your life. In a world filled with takers, the contrarian approach will ultimately lead you to a life of abundance.

It may seem counterintuitive, but the path to abundance is found through giving. You see, the funny thing about the giving path is, you don't actually lose anything. In fact, those who consistently give are the ones who ultimately get more of everything!

I know what you are thinking. If I have one cookie, and my friend has no cookies, and I give my cookie to that friend, now she has one cookie, and I have none. *So how do I have more?* It's normal for you to think this way because you've been programmed with the conventional wisdom that tells you the way to play it safe is to take and keep. But the conventional wisdom is based on a scarcity mindset. This mindset will lead you to a place of fear, causing you to think, *If I give up my cookie, I'll never have another to eat.*

By taking on a contrarian perspective, you'll come to realize the value of having an abundance mindset. This mindset allows you to understand that the world is full of cookies. In fact, there are endless varieties, flavors, and sizes of cookies. You will always have the opportunity to eat more.

Think of it this way: Eddie and a friend are sitting at lunch. Eddie has one cookie and notices his friend has none. Eddie thinks, *I can give this cookie to my friend, but then I won't have the cookie, and I really want to enjoy it.* So Eddie keeps the cookie. While chewing, he finds the taste average. Eddie also notices his friend is bummed out.

Sally is in the same situation. However, she chooses to give her cookie to her friend. Her friend's genuine excitement and sincere gratitude bring Sally more joy than the cookie's taste ever would have. Then an interesting thing happens. Two other people at the table witness what happened and realize that Sally no longer has a cookie, so they both offer Sally theirs.

Now Sally went from one cookie to no cookies to having the opportunity to enjoy *two cookies*! Sally finds herself at a crossroads. She can accept one cookie, two cookies, or neither of the cookies. Regardless of what she chooses, Sally has the one thing all humans desire in life: *control*. The decision is hers, and whichever choice she makes will now make her happy. And it all started by being a giver, understanding the contrarian approach, and having a mindset of abundance.

When I consider the ways people engage with scarcity and abundance mindsets, I notice three distinct types of people on this planet: energy vampires, energy angels, and ham sandwiches (naturally).

ENERGY VAMPIRES. A vampire sucks the blood and, ultimately, the life out of people. An energy vampire sucks the energy—specifically the happiness and good mood—out of a person. When you buy into a scarcity mindset and become a taker, the end result is inevitably becoming an energy vampire. How do you know when you are around an energy vampire? Here are the warning signs:

- It's always all about them.
- They shame you and make you feel guilty for things.
- They are surrounded by endless drama.
- They always want to one-up you.
- They diminish your problems while playing up their own.

ENERGY ANGELS. On the other hand, an angel is a good, kind soul who is always there for you, offering unconditional love and support. They're always giving out of a spirit of abundance. Here are some ways to identify them:

- They listen to you.
- They invite others to join the group.
- They apologize when they are wrong.
- They forgive you when you are wrong.
- They give up the spotlight so others can shine.
- They want nothing in return.

HAM SANDWICH. Finally, we have the ham sandwich. A ham sandwich consists of two pieces of bread, a simple, low-flavored meat, perhaps mustard or mayonnaise, and sometimes even cheese. A ham sandwich will satisfy your hunger, but it's not something that will get you excited or something you'll ever spend extra money to have. If you eat a ham sandwich, you'll think, *Meh, that was all right.* If you don't eat a ham sandwich, you'll think, *Meh, no big deal.*

What's the point, and how does this fit here? The world is full of ham-sandwich people. They stand at the crossroad and choose *nothing*. By choosing nothing, they choose not to be an energy vampire. Also, by choosing nothing, they choose not to be an energy angel. They aren't good, and they aren't bad; they are a ham sandwich—predictable and boring.

Consider for yourself which mindset you want to adopt and which path you want to take. Following the crowd will always be the easiest option. It's safe. It's secure. It's simple. Just do what everyone else does, and get what everyone else gets. Sometimes this turns out to be the right decision for you.

But remember—there's always a different path to take. Yes, it's the path less traveled. When you choose this path, those in the large group on the easy path will make fun of you and question your decision. But the race results are determined at the finish line, not the starting line. Your chances of winning the race increase when you're in a smaller group.

So lean into the abundance mindset. Be a giver—an energy angel—and seek to surround yourself with other energy angels who will run the race with you. Avoid vampires, and try your best not to be one. There's no reason to follow the conventional scarcity mindset. And finally, while it's okay to eat a ham sandwich once in a while, don't choose that as your lunch every day—and don't become one yourself.

EVERYTHING HAPPENS FOR YOU

One of my favorite parables is a story that takes place one hundred years ago about a farmer who had a son and a horse. One day the farmer's only horse ran away. His neighbors rushed over to let the farmer know how sorry they were and how unlucky he was that this happened. The farmer responded, "Perhaps," as he shrugged his shoulders.

A few days later, the horse returned, and along with it came three other wild horses. Quickly his neighbors rushed over to rejoice with the farmer. They proclaimed what a great day this was and how lucky he was to now have four horses. The farmer responded, "Perhaps," and he shrugged his shoulders.

The following day, the farmer's only son tried to ride one of the untamed horses. The horse threw him to the ground, and in doing so, the boy broke his leg. The neighbors rushed over to sympathize with the farmer, lamenting how unlucky his situation was. The farmer responded, "Perhaps," as he shrugged his shoulders once again.

Two days later, members of the army came through town, recruiting young men to fight in the war. Upon arriving at the farmer's house and seeing his son with a broken leg, they passed him by. Once again the neighbors chimed in, sharing just how lucky the farmer was. The farmer responded, "Perhaps," and he shrugged his shoulders.

Many things that happen in life will happen *for* you in some way, not simply *to* you. Rarely do we recognize that seemingly unfortunate events are actually blessings in the long term. You have to have faith, no matter what the present moment may look like.

We all experience a recency bias. This means we tend to believe that whatever events are happening in our life right now, today, at this very moment, will last forever. I'm here to remind you that nothing lasts forever. Good times will turn to bad, and bad times will turn to good. Rarely do we understand *why* at the time. During dark moments, keep the faith that bright days lie ahead, and during happy times, fully embrace the moment because those seasons come in small doses.

Stay present, and live fully in each short period of time. Understand that everything happens for a reason, though we often cannot see it or at least cannot see it yet. In the ups and downs, when friends, family, and neighbors rush to remind you how lucky or unlucky you are, take some advice from the farmer and say, "Perhaps," as you shrug your shoulders.

This is a lesson I learned for myself my senior year of high school. I was one of six football players on my team looking to play at the college level. Two of the six knew exactly where they wanted to attend college. Three others were close friends, and I went with them to visit numerous schools on recruit weekends. After a few months of visits, all four of us decided on the same college. We would all attend in the fall and continue to play football there together!

The snag came when only three of us got accepted to that college. Yup, you guessed it. *I was the one who didn't get in.* So I appealed the decision. I went and interviewed with the college's admission board, but they still said no. I was crushed. I spent the entire summer upset about it. I didn't understand why this was happening to me. It didn't feel fair.

Fast-forward to one year later. My three buddies who went to that school had all flunked out. They were more interested in what the school offered in terms of parties than studying and playing ball. I am certain that, were I accepted to that school with them, I too would have flunked out alongside them.

It's another year down the road. I was in the fall semester of junior year at my second-choice school when a blond-haired, blue-eyed freshman stepped foot on campus. Before long, we started spending time together, discovered we had a lot in common, and decided we'd date one another exclusively at the end of the school year. Yes, that pretty freshman girl is now my wife of over twenty years and the mother of my three amazing children.

When I was the only person who didn't get into that college with my buddies, I didn't understand why. My recency bias had me believing my college career would suck forever. What I didn't realize at the time is that life happens *for* you, not *to* you. After four years, I had a bachelor's degree, discovered a passion for writing, met incredible lifelong friends, and bonded with a beautiful soul with whom I will spend the rest of my days.

You will arrive at many crossroads because things didn't go the way you planned. Unfortunate events will occur, and it will seem like you have no luck. At these crossroads, you can throw a pity party and feel sorry for yourself, or you can shrug your shoulders, accept the fact that you cannot change what happened, and move forward with the faith that whatever is happening to you is happening for a reason.

Ultimately, it's all happening *for* you. When a window closes, a door opens. Changes throughout your career and in your life may seem devastating at the time, but they often lead to greater opportunities elsewhere. Be patient. Part of seeing how everything in your life happens for you involves understanding that your present circumstances won't last forever.

BLINK AND YOU'LL MISS IT

Let me challenge you with one last mindset: not only does everything in your life happen *for* you—everything in your life is *temporary*. I realize this may be difficult to fully appreciate because you've only had a short time here on earth, and you don't remember your first few years anyway. A lot of the things you've had in your life have probably been pretty constant. When you're young, everything in your life seems like an eternity, and the way things are today feel like they will be that way forever. But the truth is that nothing in life is permanent.

Every mountain your conquer will be a blip on your life's radar. Each success will be a milestone to your next one. Your finances are temporary. You won't be in the same job forever. Your body will deteriorate. Friends will come and go. Even family will come and go. And the longer you're on this planet, the faster these changes seem to come.

You may be asking, "Scott, what's the point of saying all this? It sounds a little depressing."

I'll admit it's true that the fleeting nature of reality can be scary, but let me counter by saying that understanding impermanence is actually a powerful and empowering concept with significant implications for your mindset and actions.

First, impermanence allows us to embrace change. It encourages a flexible mindset. Being open to change allows us to pivot and adapt to new circumstances, leading to growth and new opportunities. Change is a natural part of life, and resisting it only leads to frustration and stagnation. Don't run from what's difficult. Embrace change rather than resisting it. Life is full of change, but what that means is that you can be a catalyst for change too.

Second, understanding the transience of life helps us to appreciate the moment. When we know that our moments are fleeting, we're encouraged to live fully in the present. We don't wish our years away. The temporariness of life reminds us to appreciate the good times and learn from the challenging ones. When you know that you'll only have something for a limited time, you're more likely to cherish and enjoy it. It feels more special, and you're more grateful to have it.

Third, knowing that everything is temporary helps us counter our fear of failure by putting things in perspective. When we recognize that our failures are temporary, it reduces our fear of taking risks. We can be resilient in the face of failure and optimistic about the days ahead. Failures are just stepping stones to success and not permanent marks against us. They're not as big as we make them seem.

Half the battle is understanding and believing that whatever events you are experiencing at this very moment—good or bad—are only temporary. Letting go of past regrets allows you to move forward with a clear mind and a fresh perspective.

Finally, knowing that our time is short benefits us by giving us the urgency to act, seize the day, and make good on the time that we have. We're better positioned to zero in on what's truly important because we realize we don't want to waste our time on trivial things.

Don't wait for things to happen; take action to create the life you want. Whether it's changing your career, learning a new skill, or improving relationships, you have the ability to make those changes. Chase what excites and inspires you. Let go of the past, focus on growth, and be a catalyst for change. Pursue your passions before you lose that chance.

The world is filled with retirees who have everything society sees as successful. However, the one thing these retirees don't have—which money cannot buy—is *time*. Millions of millionaires would trade everything they have for the opportunity to go back in time and do it all again. You have that time. Don't waste it. Enjoy every moment.

CHAPTER FOUR

NO TURNING BACK

You don't lose if you get knocked down; you lose if you stay down.
—MOHAMMED ALI

In 1519, Hernán Cortés led a large expedition to the new world. His goal was the conquest of the Aztec Empire to capture a magnificent treasure said to be held there. Cortés and his crew made their way to Mexico. But Cortés knew some of his crew weren't totally bought into the vision. Many were exhausted after their journey to the New World, and some were even plotting to escape to Cuba in some of the ships.

To prevent this from happening, Cortés destroyed his own ships by setting them on fire. *He burned his own boats.* This sent a clear message to his army: there would be no turning back. They would either conquer the Aztec Empire or die trying. Retreat was not an option. And indeed, within two years, Cortés and his army conquered the Aztec Empire.

At some point in your life, you might have been encouraged to "burn the boats"—to commit to whatever you're doing and leave no room for a backup plan. Burning the boats forces you to a point of no return. It gives you no plan B. It creates a 100 percent psychological commitment to success. As Elizabeth Holmes said, "The minute you have a backup plan, you've admitted you're not going to succeed."

Now, let's be clear. I do not believe that burning the boats is always the right strategy for everyone or in every situation. It only applies when you are fully committed to something and willing to go "all in." It can be incredibly motivating and empowering, but it requires a significant level of confidence in your direction and a deep understanding of your goals and the path you're taking. If you lack this confidence, burning the boats can lead to unnecessary stress and potential failure because you haven't properly prepared yourself for the journey ahead.

I'll admit that the story of Cortés and his army is a harsh tale of a life-or-death risk. But the worst-case scenario for the vast majority choices you'll face in life won't be nearly as dire. Let that encourage you to be a little more willing to burn the boats as you embark on new challenges.

Over the course of my career, I've asked myself a set of questions before taking on any new challenge that I didn't feel completely ready for:

- What is the worst-case scenario here?
- Will this potentially kill me?
- Can I potentially end up in prison as a result of this?
- Will my family still love and respect me if I fail?

As long as I can live with the answers to those questions, I know I shouldn't let my fears control me. I can choose to step forward in full confidence and burn my proverbial boats. I can go all in and not look back.

Perhaps the greatest company slogan ever created came from Nike: "Just Do It." The stories of people who *could have*, *would have*, and *should have* but ultimately *didn't* are riddled with procrastination, excuses, and failure. You will never be completely ready to do anything in life. Sometimes you have to jump and figure out your plan on the way down. Remember, taking imperfect action is always better than taking no action at all because true failure happens when you don't bother to try. Your life will change forever when you stop talking about making things happen and choose to *just do it!*

Once you're confident about your direction, the benefits of 100 percent psychological commitment can indeed outweigh the benefits of having a backup plan for a number of reasons. When you commit fully without a backup plan, you eliminate distractions and excuses. Your mind becomes laser-focused on your goal, which enhances your determination and drive.

On the other hand, having a backup plan can sometimes make you complacent. You might not push yourself as hard if you know there's a safety net to catch you if you fall. By burning the boats, you remove this comfort zone, which forces you to push past your limits. That's because fully committing can provide a significant psychological boost. It reinforces your belief in your capabilities and your mission. This confidence propels you forward, even when the going gets tough. It pushes you to find creative solutions and persevere through obstacles because *failure is simply not an option.*

Without a safety net, you feel compelled to give your maximum effort. You tap into levels of resourcefulness and resilience that you might not even know you had. As a result, you can experience personal growth and a deeper sense of achievement as you reach your goals.

Throughout your life, you will encounter numerous crossroads that will demand you choose whether to take a risk or play it safe. My hope is that you'll take this persistent, all-in mentality with you through each and every one. When you come to one of these crossroads, assess your confidence by weighing your potential for loss against the benefits of burning your boats. Ask yourself the worst thing that could happen if you went all in. More often than not, you'll discover that the risk is well worth the reward. So *just do it*. Take the leap, and don't look back. Burn the boats!

DON'T QUIT

How do so many people get to the end of their lives, only to realize they aren't the person they wanted to be? The answer is shockingly simple. In fact, it's the easiest thing in the world to do. It takes no effort, zero skill, and everyone is instantly born with the ability to do it: *they quit.*

Yup, those four letters, *Q-U-I-T,* have ended more dreams, crushed more hopes, and extinguished more fires that once burned inside people's souls than you might think possible.

You start your life sprinting out of the gate with that bright flame of desire burning within you. When exciting opportunities or challenges arise in your life, you raise your hand and say, "Pick me!"

But then the work sets in. And the work isn't easy. The work never stops. There are obstacles now. You struggle and fumble. You're tested, and you fail.

And the process repeats itself. What you don't realize is that, through it all, you are outrageously, infuriatingly close to where you want to be! But you don't know that. You can't see the finish line. You're tired. You lose hope. And so you do the only thing that can prevent you from accomplishing what you started. You quit.

Please don't quit on your hopes and dreams. Anything worth having is worth working for. So please don't quit on Future You. The current version of you is already amazing. At this stage of your life, you've accomplished so much and are loved by so many—and you're only just beginning. Future You can change the world by positively impacting and inspiring all those around you. However, you cannot become the best possible version of yourself in the future if you consistently quit today.

Each time you keep a promise to yourself, you grow stronger and gain confidence. You increase love and respect for yourself. You gain the courage to make even bigger promises to yourself in the future. Not quitting builds resilience, perseverance, and a growth mindset. By pushing through challenges, you develop the strength to handle adversity, the courage to take risks, and the wisdom to learn from your mistakes. This can lead to greater achievements, a more fulfilling life, and the realization of your true potential. The process of not quitting shapes you into someone who can adapt, overcome, and thrive despite setbacks—ultimately making you into a person who is proud of their journey and accomplishments.

On the other hand, quitting diminishes your self-worth and depletes your future potential. Each time you break a promise to yourself, you chip away a piece of the Future You that you're hoping to become. Quitting can profoundly affect the kind of person you become because it reinforces a mindset of giving up when things get tough. When you quit, you avoid facing challenges, learning from failures, and pushing beyond your comfort zone. This can lead to a life of complacency, missed opportunities, and unfulfilled potential. You might end up settling for less than what you truly desire, living a life dictated by fear and the avoidance of discomfort.

So don't quit. Instead, choose to *adapt*. Take a moment to understand the difference between these two words. "To quit" is to leave a place or stop something permanently. "To adapt" is to adjust to new conditions. When you feel like quitting, understand that it's just a sign that it's time to adapt.

It isn't a bad thing to fail. Failures are stepping stones and opportunities for growth. In fact, the only kind of failure you need to avoid is the failure to try—or to keep trying. I want you to fail *and then* adapt.

Your goal—that thing you want—hasn't changed. However, the initial way you tried to get it didn't work. That doesn't mean you quit; it means you adjust your approach based on your new knowledge. It might take dozens of adaptations to finally achieve your goal—and that's okay! Adaptations color the journey.

They let us be creative. They're the fun stuff. Quitting just ends the party. So finish what you start. Future You is counting on you.

The "cookbook" to success—both personally and professionally—only has two ingredients: *consistency* and *persistency*. Be consistent. Don't spend your time chasing the latest and greatest anything. Don't jump from the empty promise of one instant success to another. Remain consistent with the proven, worthwhile habits. Slow and steady wins the race.

At the same time, be persistent. You can't just do something once or twice and say, "I tried." You have to remain resolute in your resolve. If your first two tries didn't work, try and try (and try and try) again. Persistence always pays long-term dividends.

Doors of opportunity open for those who consistently and persistently knock. I'm reminded of a story from when my son was very young that perfectly captures this truth.

During his first trip to Disney World, at the age of six, my son decided he had to have a Donald Duck hat.

And no, I'm not talking about the little blue sailor cap you've seen Donald wear. No, this was a hat that resembled the fast-talking duck himself. The cap was white like Donald's feathers. Donald's big, blue eyes rested on the forehead. And the brim was a gigantic, yellow beak. *It looked ridiculous.*

I knew he'd never wear it again. It was expensive. The temperature was outrageously hot. His mother and I had been alternating between pushing him in the stroller and carrying his brother all day. All we wanted to do was get back to the hotel room.

But there was a problem—a big problem. *He wanted that hat.*

I told him, "You can't have the hat."

"Why not?"

"Because. Now let's go."

"Because why?"

"Because I said so."

My son folded his arms, gave his best puppy-dog eyes, and cried, "I want the hat!"

"Let's gooo!" I called back.

With heels dug into the burning-hot pavement, he retorted, "I'm *not* going. I *want* the *hat!*"

At that point, my body temperature was approaching 212 degrees. My head was about to explode. Smoke may or may not have been coming out of my ears.

"*Son*, you are *not* getting that hat!" With clenched teeth, I growled, "*Let's. Go. Now!*"

"No," he huffed.

At that point, my wife broke. "Just get him the damn hat!"

So I angrily bought the stupid hat—yes, the stupid hat that he never wore again after that trip. I'll give my son one thing. He was persistent *and* consistent, and it paid off. He kept knocking, and eventually, the door of opportunity opened.

Obviously, my son's exact bargaining style doesn't always work. Often you catch more flies with honey than with vinegar—meaning that a kind approach often gets you further in life than an abrasive one. But that doesn't mean you let go of consistent, persistent effort. In the end, those are what get you to where you want to be.

Some things in life are easy to get. Others will require extended periods of effort and commitment. But everything you desire in life is worth working for. As that work becomes more difficult, monotonous, or mundane, you'll find yourself faced with the choice of either pushing forward or quitting. Quitting will always be an option. But you may not always have the ability to keep going. So whenever the opportunity presents itself, don't choose to quit.

FAIL FORWARD

Do you remember when you were growing up and some of the teachers would have a favored teacher's pet—a student who didn't care to be a little "extra" when it came to their academics?

Throughout elementary and middle school, I must admit, I proudly fit that role. I would even go so far as to help my teacher grade my classmates' tests, and I'd watch in anticipation as he'd grade mine, hoping for that glorious "100%."

I put so much pressure on myself to be absolutely perfect. You might remember from the story I shared about discovering my inner critic that when I was in fifth grade, I failed one test, and it totally rocked my world. I had perfect scores on all my math tests until the very last one. I missed *one* question, and it absolutely broke me. And that mindset continued throughout middle school. I continued to put an outrageous amount of stress on myself to perform at a high level academically, and I did.

During my first eight years of school, I was placed on a pedestal, showcased as the gold standard because my exam scores were higher than most. Then, in my freshman year of high school, *I broke down*. All the little failures—the missed points and imperfections—had gotten to my head. So *I quit*. I didn't quit school—I just quit trying.

Gone were the days of being the teacher's pet. During these last four years of school, I let my grades plummet. I was called a failure, and I believed it. Threats were made that I wouldn't be allowed to play sports due to my academics. Teachers started telling me I was not "college material." Guidance counselors stopped helping. Instead, they recommended I pursue a career as a factory worker rather than go to college.

I was the *same* person, with the *same* potential, but one thing had changed: I bought the lie that *I* was a failure, and I let that control me. I lived so long believing that failure was the worst thing possible and that I needed to be perfect to be successful. As a result, I couldn't handle failure when it inevitably came, and so

I let it consume me. It wasn't until I entered the corporate world and began to study some of the most successful entrepreneurs and business leaders in the world that I realized failure is actually *a good thing*!

Without failure, growth cannot happen. Think about that for a second. If there was only one way to do everything, and we all just did it that one way, what would ever change? Nothing. There would be no progress, no advances in medicine or technology, and no new products—just daily boredom until the day our lives finally ended.

Everything positive in the world today is the result of people who understood that failure was the key ingredient to success. Failure is only bad when it's followed by quitting. I learned that the hard way. So please learn from my mistakes. Have the strength to *fail forward*.

Failing forward is something we were born to do. You can walk today because you refused to quit when you were a baby. You failed and fell countless times in the beginning. Yet you instinctively knew to get up and try again. Then you fell, got back up, and tried again. Look at you now! You're walking all over the place and never give a second thought to how you'll put one foot in front of the other to successfully move forward.

What if walking was treated like an exam in school at the age of one? Well, you probably would have received an *F* as a grade. The teacher would have moved on to the next lesson, and you would have crawled back to your desk and been labeled a failure. But it didn't work that way then, and you shouldn't think about failure that way now.

Honestly, the rest of life isn't much different from those early years. Sure, tasks and challenges change, but our true success is ultimately determined by how many times we fall, get back up, learn from the mistake, try again, and move forward.

You'll experience certain moments in life where you've poured significant energy into preparing for a specific event. Perhaps it's a job interview, a presentation, a test, or a relationship. You'll feel ready, confident, and give it your all. *And you will fail.*

You'll then have two choices. You can put your head down, pout, and cry the entire way home—like I did in fifth grade—or you can reframe the result. Did you fail, or did you gain a better understanding of what you could have done better? Often the best solution is determined by utilizing a process of elimination. In that case, your failures are helpful because they show you what things don't work so you can discover what actually will.

Failure is essential for your success and long-term happiness in life. Embrace it. Let it be your greatest teacher. Don't let it scare you away from trying something new. Don't let it hold you down after you fall. Most importantly, don't allow failure to define you.

Failing doesn't make you a failure. It just makes you human.

OWN IT

I'm not here to brag, be boastful, or give you my résumé, but I am proud of a few things I managed to accomplish by the time I graduated high school. One such accomplishment was ranking in the top fifty in my high school class.

Granted, I was number 49, and my class only had seventy-one graduates. (I quit trying, remember?) So I was at the top—of the bottom third. But hey, it was my group of students that actually made the top two-thirds possible!

All jokes aside, high school was a struggle for me. You've had struggles at times throughout your journey too—whether in school, sports, arts, relationships, or the like.

Whenever we struggle or even fail in certain areas, we have a choice. Option 1 is to point fingers and blame others. We identify external circumstances that held us back. We come up with an explanation as to why it's not ultimately our fault.

As a student, I excelled at picking apart the list of top students in my class and identifying all of the reasons I thought they performed better than me. Tara was naturally gifted from kindergarten. Beth didn't play any sports, so she had extra time for schoolwork. Joe's parents were doctors, and they spent a lot of money on tutors for him. The list went on and on.

Or you can choose option 2: *owning your own results*. To do that, you have to understand that every result in your life is directly influenced by all the choices you have made leading up to it. Blaming others is simply a ploy to excuse yourself.

The one thing that was never on my list of reasons that people outperformed me was *me*! I never admitted that my biggest problem was *my* lack of commitment to school—that *I* had quit. I enjoyed sports, hanging with buddies, spending time with my girlfriend, and going to the gym. I chose not to get the grades Tara, Beth, and Joe got. Then I justified my excuses so I'd feel better about my choices.

Here's my challenge to you: choose option 2. Own everything in your life—the good and the bad. Don't hide from what's ugly. Don't run away from what was scary. Don't find excuses as to why something didn't turn out as you had hoped. Own it. Own it all.

While you can't control everything that happens to you, you can control how you respond to those events through your attitude, actions, and effort. In a sense, external events can impact your results. There are factors beyond your control that can influence the outcomes you experience. However, this doesn't mean you should shift the blame away from yourself or diminish your sense of ownership.

First, you need to own the level of preparation and the choices you made leading up to the event. While you can't predict every challenge, being proactive and making informed decisions can significantly influence your outcomes. If things don't go as planned, reflect on what you could have done differently and how you can improve moving forward.

Second, own the process of learning from every experience. External events, especially the challenging ones, provide valuable lessons. Instead of blaming external factors, focus on what you can learn and how you can grow. This mindset turns every experience into an opportunity for improvement and resilience.

Finally, owning your results means acknowledging that, despite these external influences, *you are responsible* for how you *navigate* and *respond* to them. Whether it's a setback, a failure, or an unexpected obstacle, your response to any given external event is within your control. Your attitude, actions, and effort in the face of adversity are what shape your results in the long run. Even if the event wasn't your fault, how you deal with it is entirely up to you.

You might be saying, "Scott, that's a lot for one person to take on. What hope do I have for the future if I have to own all my past failures?"

My encouragement would be to understand that your past does not determine your future; each present moment does.

Who you were yesterday doesn't determine who you will be tomorrow. The choices you make today will decide that.

Yes, I used to be a poor student. Today I'm a world-class learner. That's a conscious decision that I make each day. You can't change your past, but it's all behind you now. Each new day, focus on what lies ahead. Your future will be determined by the decisions you make *today*. Some will be good, others will be bad, but they'll all be yours to own.

Keep learning—especially from your failures. Your education doesn't end when you graduate from high school. Challenge yourself to be a lifelong learner. You need to learn if you want to earn. You may think you aren't smart enough to do something (which may be the case at that very moment), but it doesn't have to be that way forever. Nobody starts by knowing everything. As you learn, give yourself permission to suck at new things. No one masters anything immediately either.

Along the way, your life will be filled with moments where you wish you could have a redo. You'll speak words you wish you hadn't. You'll act in ways you wish you didn't. Your missteps will bring you to yet another crossroad, where you'll have two choices. You can either lie about your failure, make excuses, and cast blame—or you can own it.

We are all flawed as humans. We all make mistakes. It's impossible to pretend that we're not and that we don't. So ask for forgiveness, learn, and move on. No matter what, always choose the path of ownership.

FORGIVE YOURSELF

Owning your mistakes and asking for forgiveness gets you halfway, but there's another side to the forgiveness coin. *You have to be able to forgive yourself too.* Just as holding a grudge against others festers negative emotions inside of you, so too will refusing to forgive yourself for personal wrongdoings. People will forgive you for your mistakes, but it means nothing unless you're willing to forgive yourself and move on too. You need to remember that you're human too.

It was just before sunset on a hot evening in August. My best friend Chris and I—both thirteen years old at the time—were riding our bikes around town. We passed the basketball courts in the park when a well-known school bully (a senior on the football team whom I'll call "Meathead") yelled for us to come over to the courts. My friend Chris was the biggest kid in our freshman class, but he was nowhere near as big as seventeen-year-old Meathead, who wanted to show off in front of his crew.

"Hey, you think you're tough because you're the biggest kid on the freshman football team?" Meathead asked.

Chris sheepishly answered, "No," with his head down.

"Do you think you're tougher than me?" Meathead repeated.

Chris said, "No way." This time he looked over to me and said, "We're out of here!" He hopped on his bike and began to pedal away.

Unfortunately, he didn't pedal fast enough. Meathead sprinted after him, grabbed Chris by the back of his T-shirt, and pulled him off the bike.

"Don't insult me by leaving before I was done talking to you," he yelled while picking up Chris's bike and slamming it to the ground.

The bike was lying next to Chris when Meathead started jumping up and down on it, destroying the tires. Chris got up to stop him but was quickly pushed back to the ground.

Suddenly, Meathead looked at me and asked, "How about you, little guy? Do you have something to say?"

My head went numb, and a tingling sensation ran through my fingers and toes. I was so scared I couldn't even speak. So I ran! Well, I didn't run, but I pedaled my bike as fast as possible, fully expecting Meathead to be chasing behind. But he wasn't.

What I didn't consider was that I was leaving Chris alone, laughed at, and forced to carry his broken bike back home. When it hit me, I was so mad at myself for running. I felt like I was the worst friend in the world. I couldn't sleep all night, fearing my best friend would never talk to me again.

But that's not what best friends do.

That next morning I went to Chris's house to apologize.

He chuckled and asked, "What are you sorry about?"

"I left you. I didn't stick up for you. I just let it happen and ran away scared."

He raised his eyebrow and laughed. "Dude, he would have killed you if you said something. He'd have broken your ribs by poking you with two fingers. I'm actually glad he didn't get the satisfaction of punking us both."

Clearly, my friend forgave me, but I couldn't forgive myself. I replayed that day over and over in my mind. I kept getting angry about all the things I could have done or should have done but didn't. I started hanging out with my best friend less because I was convinced that, deep down, he was really mad at me.

In fact, it was close to half a decade later—during our senior year of high school—when I brought that story up to Chris as we reminisced about our ups and downs prior to graduation.

He looked at me and said, "You need to let that go, my man! I didn't care then, and I don't care now."

At that moment, I realized that my inability to forgive myself for how I acted one day caused me five years of unnecessary stress and anxiety.

Unfortunately, most people put themselves through this kind of unnecessary suffering. We spend all sorts of time and energy worrying about things we cannot change rather than being willing to show a little kindness and grace to ourselves.

People often have a hard time letting go of past mistakes because they don't want to forgive themselves. For some people, it's rooted in perfectionism. Many people hold themselves to extremely high standards. When they fall short, they struggle to forgive themselves because they feel they should have done better. They have a hard time accepting mistakes as a natural part of growth.

Others have a hard time with self-forgiveness due to the voices of SIN. Our inner critic can be incredibly harsh. Negative self-talk magnifies our mistakes and makes us feel unworthy of forgiveness. This internal dialogue reinforces feelings of guilt and shame, making it harder to have compassion for oneself.

Whatever the reason, allow yourself the grace needed to forgive yourself. You've heard that holding a grudge against someone else only hurts you—but the same is true when it comes to holding a grudge against yourself! Beating yourself up over mistakes won't change what happened. The only way to deal with the past is to learn from it, forgive yourself, and move on.

The next time you are in the car, take a look at the front windshield. It's extremely large and provides a tremendous view of the road ahead of you. Then take a look at the rearview mirror affixed to the windshield. That mirror is about 95 percent smaller than the front windshield. Use that size ratio as a guide for your life, letting 95 percent of your focus be on what's ahead and only letting 5 percent go to what's behind. You can't live your life in the rearview mirror. Use the past as a guide, but be sure you're living in the present. Otherwise, you'll miss the precious moments happening now.

Countless moments in your life will come and go. Inevitably, you'll look back with some regrets, wishing you had or hadn't done or said certain things. There will be moments when you'll have to ask for forgiveness. Once you've spent some time in self-reflection and learned from your misstep, it's time to *forgive yourself too*. It's either the path of carrying baggage from your past or walking in freedom. Don't hold yourself back. Make the choice to forgive yourself and keeping moving forward. There's no turning back now.

CHAPTER FIVE

WATCH FOR INNER WORK OPPORTUNITIES

The weak can never forgive. Forgiveness is the attribute of the strong.

—GANDHI

You're human, but so is everyone else. Business executives, teachers, religious leaders, construction workers, accountants, local volunteers, and yes, even your favorite Contrarian Narrator—everyone you meet is flawed. To meet a living, breathing human is to meet an imperfect work in progress.

You know those wild, sometimes seemingly crazy thoughts in your head? *Others have them too.* You know that doubting, critical, negative voice that tells you that you don't belong and that you're not good enough? *Others have that too.* You remember that time you wish you hadn't said or done that thing? *Others have those same regrets too.* You know that time you had an opportunity to do something that you really wanted to do, but fear held you back, and you didn't? *Others have had those same missed opportunities too.*

We tend to think we are the only ones with specific struggles. Beware of the lying nature of your brain! It will lead you to believe that other people have things all figured out, that things just come easy to them, or that they have more opportunities than you do. Well, they don't. They are flawed humans—imperfect works in progress—just like you.

Living in a world where everyone brings a little mess to the table creates infinite opportunities for inner work. It can be challenging as you learn to navigate life in the context of such imperfection. But you can't fix everyone else. You're only responsible for one person: *you*. So let's start there by looking at some of the areas where inner work is most critical.

FORGIVING OTHERS

Oftentimes in life, you'll be on the receiving end of someone else's imperfections. They will say things to you that they'll wish they hadn't. They will do things they'll wish they didn't. It's likely that they too have things going on in their life *that you can't see* and *that you may not know about.*

When someone wrongs you, there are a couple of common responses. One is that you may internalize their wrongdoing. You turn the blame on yourself and believe that what *they did* is somehow *your* fault. You might struggle with a bit of an inferiority complex and assume that if something went wrong, it was probably on you somehow. But here is what I want you to remember: when someone does you wrong, *it's them, not you*.

Or let's say somebody did you wrong, lied to you, disrespected you, stole from you, cheated on you, just ticked you off, or generated any other upsetting emotion within you.

Perhaps your immediate response is not to blame yourself but to get upset or angry at them. *How dare they? What were they thinking?* Your instinct will be to play the victim. You'll ask yourself, *Why me?* You'll tell yourself that you didn't deserve whatever they said or did. And guess what? You'll probably be right. Frequently, your feelings will be justified.

But at this point, you have two options. You can forgive and forget and move on in a healthy fashion, or you can hold a grudge. The grudge is the easier decision. I mean, *you were in the right!* Shouldn't they be coming to apologize to you?

But holding in those feelings of resentment only punishes the most important person in your world: *you*. Don't build a life around easy solutions to complex problems. Instead, deal with it the way it should be dealt with. Forgive those who do you wrong, and set yourself free emotionally. Don't take other people's mistakes personally. Allow them the opportunity to apologize or take it back. And if they choose not to, then it's on you to forgive them for their mistakes anyways.

Remember, holding a grudge only hurts you. As Drake once said, "Grudges are a waste of perfect happiness. Laugh when you can, apologize when you should, and let go of what you can't change."

Even if you cannot verbally speak the words "I forgive you" to someone who did you wrong, type them. Perhaps that's a text or any other form of typed communication. If you prefer to write the words out on paper, do it. Even if you cannot deliver that paper to the person, still write the words. It's a start. Even if it's just forgiving the person in your own mind and wishing them happiness going forward, think it and mean it.

Grudges are a storage locker for your anger and ill will toward others. Nothing inside that locker will bring you happiness or move you forward in life, so throw it all away. The longer you let that locker sit in your brain and soul, the less space you'll have for more important things. Also, the longer it's there, the greater chance will be of it opening up in the future.

You are too amazing to carry pain from the past. *Forgiveness* will set you free and allow you to enjoy the view from life's high road. Nothing will free your mind and soul faster than forgiving others, even when they may not deserve it.

I understand that you won't want to do this at times. I get that much of what I've shared in this chapter thus far is unnatural and difficult. But that's why I wrote this book and why I strongly encourage you to be aware of and work to improve in these areas. Simply put, you can be the one who is "right" all the time and play the victim who was "wronged," or you can be the bigger person who moves on to bigger things—but you can't do both.

Now, I do want to add just one caveat.

Let me strongly encourage you to reflect on this ancient proverb throughout your life: "Fool me once, shame on you. Fool me twice, shame on me." Read that again and again and again. Allow the depth of those words to sink in. Yes, everyone is a flawed human, and everyone makes mistakes. However, there is a big difference between a onetime mistake and a consistent pattern of bad choices.

If you find yourself in a situation where you are a victim of any sort of abuse, you can still find forgiveness in your heart, but you may need to eliminate that person from your life. There is a big difference between "Oops, I messed up" and becoming the consistent target of somebody's anger and abuse. Yes, humans are flawed. Yes, all humans deserve forgiveness. But that doesn't exclude the reality that there are some humans from whom you just need to distance yourself for your own emotional and physical health and safety.

People can only cause you long-term pain if you allow them to. Always give people the opportunity to prove to you who they are. Once you know who they truly are—keeping in mind that their actions speak louder than their words—decide if they are worth being around. Adopt a "you can't hurt me" mentality.

You know who you are—you're an amazing human. You love and respect others. You truly care about others. You are working to improve yourself and help leave the world around you just a little better than how it was given to you. You understand that you are flawed, and now you understand that everyone else is too. When others do or say undesirable things to you, you understand that *it's them, not you*. Once you forgive them and move on—either with or without them in your life—they can no longer hurt you.

ROOTING FOR YOUR COMPETITION

Another piece of the inner work puzzle is learning how to root for others. We live in a society that loves to compete. I love to compete, and I bet you do too. Competition is healthy. It's our measuring stick for where we are now, and it shines a light on areas we need to improve so we are more prepared for future competitions.

But I'll share with you a trick that helps you overcome the discouraging side of competition. There's actually a way that you can ensure you'll never lose: *root for your competition*.

Sounds silly, right? But think about it. If your goal is to learn and grow from the experience, you free yourself up to cheer for others. You're drawing from your abundance mindset to be a *giver*, not just a *taker*. Remember, you don't lose—you learn.

Rooting for your competition actually benefits you in more ways than one. When you're not bogged down by jealousy or fear of failure, you can focus on growth and improvement. What's more, cheering for the competition can inspire you to set higher goals and work harder. It can provide insights into different approaches and strategies that you might not have otherwise considered and drive innovation and excellence as a result. When you root for your competition, you are more likely to view your competitors as benchmarks and sources of inspiration rather than threats. This mindset can push you to strive for your best while maintaining a positive and constructive outlook.

What's more, rooting for your competition is beneficial because it encourages working together. Cheering for your competitors can open up opportunities for collaboration and networking. By acknowledging the strengths and achievements of others, you can build mutually beneficial relationships that may lead to partnerships, shared knowledge, and new opportunities. Of course, it's important to think for yourself and adopt a contrarian perspective when necessary, but that doesn't mean you can't also appreciate and learn from others.

Of course, I'm not saying you should let your competition win. You should want to win too! When that gun goes off and the race begins, run with every intention of crossing that finish line first! But after the race—after all the focused preparation and giving all your energy and effort to the event—if you don't win, only allow yourself to be upset for a short time.

You didn't really lose. Sure, in the example of a singular race, one person will win, and everyone else will lose. But in the context of life, there are many races throughout each day—so losing one does not make you a "loser." Don't forget that personal growth and improvement are the ultimate goals. When you root for others and focus on bettering yourself, you eliminate the zero-sum game mentality.

Success becomes about continuous learning and improvement rather than just winning and losing. If your aim is self-improvement and you're inspired by others' achievements, you can't be "beaten" because every experience contributes to your growth. As long as you're growing, you can rest in the knowledge that you're winning in the end.

Rooting for the competition can extend well beyond the world of sports. Here are just a few of the ways that you can root for the competition in various spheres of life:

- **ACADEMIC SETTING.** If you're in a competitive academic program, you might support your classmates by sharing study materials, offering to study together, or helping each other understand difficult concepts.

- **WORKPLACE.** In a professional environment, rooting for the competition can mean congratulating a coworker on a successful project or promotion. It can also involve collaborating with colleagues to improve overall team performance, sharing best practices, and providing constructive feedback to help them grow.

- **BUSINESS.** If you own a small business, supporting other local businesses can create a strong community network. This can involve cross-promotions, attending each other's events, and referring customers when appropriate.

- **CREATIVE FIELDS.** In creative industries like writing, music, or art, rooting for the competition means appreciating and promoting the work of your peers. Sharing their work on social media, attending their events, and collaborating on projects can help create a supportive and inspiring creative community.

- **TECHNOLOGY AND INNOVATION.** In tech fields, supporting competitors can look like open-sourcing your projects, contributing to community-driven initiatives, and participating in collaborative events like hackathons.

- **NONPROFITS AND SOCIAL CAUSES.** In the nonprofit sector, organizations often work toward similar goals. Rooting for the competition can involve partnering with other nonprofits for joint events, sharing resources, and promoting each other's campaigns to amplify the impact of your collective efforts.

- **EDUCATION.** As a teacher or educator, supporting fellow educators by sharing lesson plans, teaching strategies, and classroom management tips can help improve the overall quality of education and fosters a positive and collaborative environment.

For years I saw others in the training-and-development space as my "competition." I avoided them and became angry when people chose them over me. It was a scarcity mindset. But once I made the shift to collaboration, I began reaching out to competitors, asking to chat. I discovered that most were like-minded, really good people. We shared the same goals and visions.

Once the relationships were formed, we began brainstorming new ideas and ways to improve our businesses. We guested on each other's podcasts and even did joint trainings together. I'd even publicly promote and endorse their services on my social platforms.

The results? We all stepped up our games, improved our results, and better served our customers—which was always our main focus to begin with. I've learned that collaboration happens at the top, while competition is at the bottom.

Take a minute to think about how you can bring the principle of rooting for the competition into your own life. In what spheres of life do you find yourself falling back into the me-vs.-them mentality? Don't let it stay that way. Be intentional about finding ways to celebrate others' victories. As long as you're rooting for the competition, you never have to be afraid to lose.

LEVERAGING ANXIETY

Another very human struggle that's especially prevalent in teenagers is anxiety. Let me start by saying that anxiety is natural and normal. It's not something to hide from or be ashamed of. But it *is* powerful, and it has the potential to either be a force for good or for harm in your life. That's why it's vital you do the inner work to know how to talk about, think about, and respond to anxiety as it arises in your life.

I've battled anxiety since I was your age. I've experienced various versions and levels of it throughout my life. For years I was embarrassed and ashamed of it. I felt it made me weak or that something was wrong with me because everyone else seemed fine. So I did the worst thing a person struggling with anxiety can do: I hid it.

Perhaps anxiety isn't something you are dealing with now, but I can assure you that it will be present in your life in the future, and that's okay. Learn about it, learn to welcome it, and most importantly, learn how to talk about it.

A 2020 article by *Harvard Business Review* reports that anxiety is the most common mental illness, affecting more than 40 million adults each year. Close to 30 percent of Americans experience clinical anxiety at some point in their lives. According to the Institute for Health Metrics and Evaluation, an estimated 284 million people had an anxiety disorder in 2017, making it the most prevalent mental disorder worldwide.

Why is this? You have to understand that the standard equipment installed in your brain at conception is outdated. This is no fault of your own, but as the world has evolved, our brains have remained primitive. The primary purpose of your brain is to keep you safe and run efficiently.

During the era of cave people, this was great. They slept or rested for twenty hours a day, then hunted and gathered for the rest of their time. While out and about, if they heard movement in a bush, their brain sent a message of fear, creating awareness of a potential sabertooth tiger.

Fortunately, the chances of us being attacked by a tiger have significantly decreased! However, we have kept the same brain, and it's now working on overload. Instead of resting for twenty hours, it seems like we are on the run for twenty hours each day. Instead of sending fear cues to keep us safe, it sends us fear signals when facing things like homework, projects, assignments, bills, schedules, and our health. What does it all add up to? *Anxiety.*

But anxiety comes in two forms: *facilitating* and *debilitating.*

Facilitating anxiety can work as a positive force within you. When you learn to recognize and harness it, you become more focused and energetic before a big event, such as a presentation, performance, meeting, or date.

Debilitating anxiety is facilitating anxiety's drunk brother nobody wants at the party. It creates intense levels of fear about everyday situations to the point that you cannot even do certain things or function at all. For me, this commonly occurred when I was in small spaces or felt trapped. My entire college career, I couldn't sit in a classroom without windows because I freaked out. To this day, I struggle to sit in a car on the highway because I feel trapped.

But facilitating anxiety, on the other hand, is actually capable of doing some good. I remember also experiencing this in college in my public speaking class. I had done some research on anxiety and began learning how to cope with it. I taught myself to recognize this scary emotion and translate it into excitement. Prior to my big speech in class, I performed a series of deep-breathing exercises and allowed myself to get motivated by the rush of nerves. I turned my anxious feelings into the fuel I needed to carry me through, and I walked out of my presentation still riding that high.

More than anything, my wish for you is that you learn how to live with your anxieties. Do not allow anxiety to keep you from trying and trying and trying again. Whatever is wildly important to you, do it. Harness your anxiety. Use it as a reminder that you are doing difficult but necessary work.

Understanding anxiety and harnessing its positive powers will serve you well throughout your life. Understand that everyone deals with anxiety; that, regardless of its intensity, it's nothing to be ashamed of; and that it's essential to have somebody to talk to about it.

Inevitably, the time will come in your life when you are suddenly derailed by angst, worry, and overwhelming feelings. You will feel short of breath, begin to sweat, and notice your heart pounding through your chest. Anxiety can hit you quickly. It's often triggered instantly, like a light switch turning on. Unfortunately, it's not as easy to turn off.

When this happens, take note of it, and understand this is a temporary state. I'd also recommend focusing on your breathing by implementing a technique that soldiers and police officers use before entering life-or-death situations called *combat breathing*.

The technique is simple. Breathe in through your nose for a three-second count, hold your breath for a three-second count, and exhale through your mouth for a three-second count. If you are in a situation where you can do this with your eyes closed, then close them. If not, no big deal. Repeat this nine-second breath pattern as long as it takes to decrease your heart rate. In through the nose for three, hold for three, and out through the mouth for three.

Remember the E + R = O formula here: *Event* plus *Response* equals *Outcome*. We cannot control the event (our anxiety), but we can control our responses through awareness, breath work, or talking it through with somebody. If you do, the outcome will be just fine. In fact, you'll be stronger for having worked through it.

SOCIAL MEDIA

One of the biggest minefields for teens to navigate in our world today is social media. Welcome to the land of make-believe! Here in social media land, influencers use filters to improve their appearance in an effort to impress people they don't like. They spend money they don't have to buy things they don't want just to post them on social media in an effort to "wow" people who could care less about them. In social media land, the goal is to hide your imperfections. As a result, inner work opportunities abound.

Social media is a highlight reel of people's lives—quite literally. It offers only the very best moments of somebody's day. What you don't see are the events happening behind the scenes that lead up to those moments.

As a result, social media becomes the ultimate comparison trap. No wonder nearly a third of teenagers have an anxiety disorder! When you're constantly seeing the curated lives of others brought to you daily by an algorithm designed to allure you, it's hard not to compare.

But comparing yourself to others is never wise, and comparing yourself to false perceptions of others only lowers your self-esteem. Comparison is the thief of joy, and comparison to an impossibly perfect, false image of someone else is even more so.

Unfortunately, as long as we're being constantly inundated by the comparison trap of social media, happiness will be in short supply. Our tendency as humans is to determine our happiness by relative comparison. It's why people are more likely to choose to have an average income if their neighbors make less than them than they are to choose to have more money but with even wealthier neighbors.

So what's the solution to this comparison trap? *Run your own race.* Don't judge others who look, act, and believe differently than you. Don't be jealous of those who seem to have everything you want. While you can love and support others running their races, you can untimately only control what's happening in your own.

Yes, I'm on socials, and I realize that in today's day and age, you almost have to be. But when a product has no financial cost, just know that means, *you are the product.*

You may believe that social media is a solid downtime activity or a way to relax and take your mind off your problems. But the reality is that it's creating more problems than you may realize. Social media was created to own, control, and manipulate you. There's a reason one of Facebook's inventors, Sean Parker, has become a "conscientious objector" on social media, saying, "God only knows what it's doing to our children's brains."

Take active steps to tether yourself to the real world. Limit your social media usage to less than an hour each day. Build in *detox blocks*, where you totally eliminate social media for a day or two at a time. Not only will this reduce your anxiety by keeping you away from the comparison trap, but it will also take your eyes off content specifically placed there to manipulate your emotions. By limiting and, at times, eliminating social media, you will be more present throughout your day to see things that are real.

In place of digital distractions, create healthy distractions. These are things that require your full attention and complete focus. When you engage in these, you stop focusing on the negative, and you're enabled to detach and recharge. It's like a breath of fresh air for your brain, and you can finally refresh. Examples of healthy distractions include kickboxing, dancing, playing with kids, puzzling, painting, building or fixing something, meditating, and so on.

At least thirty minutes of your day should be set aside for these kind of life-giving activities that are engaging but that don't add negativity to your life. Otherwise, you're more susceptible to the dangers of stress and burnout.

Thousands of amazing places exist on this planet for you to experience and enjoy in this life you've been given. My ask is that you don't waste it all in social media land, the land of make-believe.

BE REAL, AVOID COMPARISON, DITCH GOSSIP

BE REAL. I have 5,000 "friends" on social media. If I ran into all of them at the store this weekend, 4,327 wouldn't even take two seconds to say, "Hey, how are you?" Some *friends*, right? Yet when I post a picture on social media, I get mad when they don't like it. Do you know why they don't like it? Because most of them don't even like me!

Brace yourself—because this one is going to sting. Eight out of ten of your *friends* on social media don't like you enough to say, "Hey, how are you?" when they see you in the real world.

You know why? Because social media is not real. It's a robot-created universe driven by algorithms designed to tick you off and then suck you back in, only to tick you off again. It's a land of make-believe, filled with real humans using you like a lab rat by capitalizing on your strongest emotional triggers to drive up engagement.

My advice is this: learn how to be real. And before you ask—no, I'm not referring to the social media platform.

Don't chase *likes*. You will know who your true friends are once you take a break from social media. They are the people still calling, texting, and wanting to hang out with you. Your real friends are those who know everything about you and still love everything about you. That's the kind of real-world approval you should seek.

There was no social media when I grew up, but there was still a strong desire for social acceptance and approval. This led me to do many things I normally wouldn't do in an effort to impress people who didn't truly like me. Learn from my experience. Identify your real friends, and leave the rest in the land of make-believe.

AVOID COMPARISON. Another key element is to avoid the comparison trap. Comparison creates unhappiness within us. Theodore Roosevelt once said, "Comparison is the thief of joy." In nearly every area of your life where you find unhappiness, you will find comparison. So to experience happiness, you must eliminate comparison.

Social media has taken this unhappy issue of comparison and put it on steroids. When we see somebody at a fancy restaurant, on an exotic trip, or out golfing with buddies, we can't help but stack it up against what we've got going on—and usually, ours seems a lot less exciting. It's not that their actions make us unhappy, rather that our incessant need to compare drains the joy out of whatever we are doing at that moment.

If you are feeling stressed out, unsuccessful, or unhappy, this is likely the result of you comparing the success of others or the success you've personally experienced in the past to your current situation.

The solution is awareness. Be aware of what is causing you this unhappiness, and force yourself to eliminate the comparisons. Embrace the moment you're in now. The perceived happiness and success of others should have no bearing on your present situation. As Zen Shin so artfully put it, "A flower does not think of competing with the flower next to it. It just blooms."

The only person you should ever compare yourself to is the person you were yesterday. How you look, your job title, your bank account, your clothes, and the car you drive should never be compared to anyone else. The only thing worth comparing to is the you that lived yesterday. Ask yourself, "Am I a better version of myself today than I was yesterday?" If your answer is yes, everything else will fall into place over time.

Root for others to live their best life, and help them do so. Celebrate with others when they succeed. However, under no circumstances should you *compare* what they have, where they are now, and how they live to your present life. We each have our storylines with our own heroes and villains. Whichever chapter the story of your life is currently on, embrace it. Your story is unique. Celebrate that. Don't get brought down by comparing it to others.

DITCH GOSSIP. Finally, just as you shouldn't compare your life to others, you shouldn't gossip about them either. Trust me, gossip is the enemy of progress. You can spend your time speaking poorly of others; or you can be a kind, compassionate, loving human. But you don't get to do both. This is a lesson I learned the hard way.

"Hey, what's the deal with Mark?" I asked this about our boss, Mark, to a coworker over the phone one day while at my first job out of college.

"I don't know. What do you mean?" my coworker replied.

"Well, he's been a real jerk recently. I do everything he asks of me all of the time, and then when I ask him for one favor, he tells me no," I explained.

Little did I know, my coworker had answered my call *on speakerphone.*

The next voice I heard was *not* my coworker's. It was Mark's.

"Hey, Scott, this is 'Mark the Jerk.' You know, the guy who always tells you no."

I got a lump in my throat and felt a tingle in my stomach as my face turned red and my heart began to accelerate.

From that day on, my relationship with Mark was never the same. I violated a trust agreement by gossiping behind his back. Going forward, this left Mark wondering how many other people I talked to that way about him when he wasn't around.

This taught me a valuable lesson—one I'll stress with you here so you don't make the same mistake. Nothing positive comes from gossip. Only the weak speak poorly about those who are not present to defend themselves. If you would be embarrassed and ashamed to have the person you are speaking about hear what you are saying—the way I was when Mark replied—then don't speak those words.

Furthermore, don't pile on when others are gossiping. And while saying nothing is better than piling on, it's still not the best option. The best option is to encourage others to stop. Don't let your silence imply approval.

Whenever you're faced with a situation where you don't appreciate, like, or support another person's actions, words, or point of view, you have two options. You can let it be known to anyone who will listen how much you despise the person not in the room. Or you can say nothing to anyone who isn't the person you have the problem with. If you feel compelled to speak your mind, pick up the phone or visit the person, and have a conversation face-to-face.

Trust me, taking the time to do the inner work is well worth the investment, so watch for inner work opportunities. Be real, avoid comparison, and ditch gossip.

CHAPTER SIX

FUEL FOR THE JOURNEY

Good health is a crown on the well person's head that only the ill can see.
—ROBIN SHARMA

At various stages of your life, you will have teachers, coaches, mentors, bosses, coworkers, friends, family, most likely a significant other, and perhaps even children of your own. You'll have various feelings on different levels for all of them. However, none of those people will be more important than *you*. Your mindset needs to be that you are Priority One. This is because when you consistently show up as the best version of yourself, you inspire those around you to become better versions of themselves too.

You may be thinking, *Wow! That sounds incredibly selfish.*

Well, I thought the same thing when I initially learned about this concept too.

It was during my very first time on an airplane. I was with my dad, and I was clearly nervous because I had never been in an aluminum tube flying through the sky before. I paid close attention to the pre-flight safety instructions (obviously). The flight attendant explained that if the cabin lost pressure, oxygen masks would drop down from above. Adults traveling with small children should place the oxygen mask over their own nose and mouth before assisting their children.

Wait, what? Did they just instruct the adults to put their needs ahead of ours—their own children?

Yes, they did. And here's why. If the adults took care of the children first and, in doing so, lost oxygen and fainted, how much help would they be to those children going forward? But by having the adults take care of themselves first, only then would they have the capacity to actually help their children.

You can't ignore your needs. If you want a lifestyle that you can actually sustain, you have to take care of yourself. Neglecting self-care can lead to burnout, which hampers your ability to be effective in your personal and professional life. Ensuring you are well rested and healthy means you can be more productive and present. Remember to stay focused on the long game, not the short-term stressors.

At the same time, taking care of yourself ensures that you have the energy, health, and mental clarity to support those around you well into the future. Moreover, taking care of yourself can benefit others because you're modeling the importance of maintaining one's health and well-being, which can inspire those around you to adopt similar practices.

Some people squirm at the idea of self-care because they don't know what it really is. Oftentimes self-care gets a bad rap because it's conflated with self-indulgence, avoiding challenges, and isolation.

But this is making self-care into something it's not. The kind of self-care I'm describing focuses on your physical, mental, emotional, and spiritual health.

To take care of your physical health, it's important to maintain regular exercise, balanced nutrition, and adequate sleep. To support yourself mentally, try your hand at activities that stimulate your mind, such as reading, doing puzzles, listening to podcasts, or learning new skills. You can care for your emotional health by doing activities that nurture your soul, like spending time with loved ones, devoting time to hobbies, or going to therapy. Finally, you can feed your spiritual health by engaging in practices that provide inner peace and fulfillment, such as meditation, prayer, mindfulness, or practicing sabbath (a weekly day of rest).

However you decide to implement self-care, make sure you do it in a way that sticks. Prioritize your needs, create routines, set boundaries, and seek support so that your resolve to take care of yourself doesn't leave the picture when life starts to get busy. Don't let self-care become another New Year's resolution left by the wayside.

Take the concept of self-care with you throughout your life. Taking care of yourself first increases your ability to lead, inspire, and improve those around you. Meanwhile, you are patiently moving toward the best possible version of Future You.

Self-care is not selfish. In fact, giving others the best possible version of you is the greatest gift you can offer the world.

YOUR PERSONAL BATTERY

Take a look at the battery life on your smartphone. Is it fully charged? I doubt it. But you're not too worried. You know you'll be able to charge it whenever you need. In fact, maybe you're even charging it right now.

But let's say we are in a new city, and we are going to explore during the morning and then get bused an hour up the road to hike some scenic trails all afternoon. At no point along our journey will you be able to charge your phone. However, you'll want to use your phone on our way back home that evening. When we leave in the morning, your phone is 100 percent charged. All day long, you have to limit your usage to conserve energy and preserve the battery life.

Your emotional energy tank—your personal battery—is no different. Each time you get upset or allow something to bother you, little energy is drained from your battery. It is no different from leaving an app open or downloading a large video. Those actions will continuously drain your cell phone battery, even if it's in your pocket. Eventually, they'll wear down your phone's battery health, and it will no longer be able to hold a good charge.

Holding grudges and not forgiving others works the same way. In the last chapter, we discussed how learning to forgive is an opportunity for inner work. More than that, it's also necessary for you to be able to take care of yourself.

Every choice we make either charges or drains our personal battery life. When you choose not to forgive, you're left feeling angry, unsettled, and raw inside. You may replay the incident or argument over and over, allowing it to take up valuable headspace. Or your bitterness may stay on a slow burn, and you'll end up wanting to get back at the other person out of spite or revenge.

But all these feelings are energy drainers and time wasters. They keep you from being the best version of yourself and wear you down day by day, year by year.

What's the alternative? I would argue it's gratitude. The connection between grudges and gratitude may not be apparent at first, but the reality is *you can't be hateful when you're grateful*. What's more, when you're grateful, you're actually recharging your battery!

When angry emotions set in, don't ignore them. Be intentional to recognize when they show up so you're able to respond to them well. Indicators include increased heart rate, shaking hands, shortness of breath, and tingling in your stomach. Use these as warning signs flashing in front of you. If you pursue that anger, your battery will drain, forcing you to find a charging station.

But if you pause, think about the situation, and reframe it, you're choosing to conserve your personal battery life. Consistently taking one deep breath during a three-second pause will change the direction of your life. You'll be able to shift your perspective and respond to what's bothering you from a better position.

We often can't see the lessons in difficult moments as they are happening. But if you take a break to reflect, you'll be giving yourself the best possible education. View every moment in your life—whether good or bad—as what it truly is: a blessing. Even if it's something bothersome, there's good you can take from it. Every trial you face will grow your perseverance and endurance, bolstering the strength of Future You.

The more positives you find in each situation, the less negative effect it has on your energy tank. The quicker you can make peace with a situation and move on, the longer your battery remains charged.

You already have all the gifts required to succeed within you. Your mission is to activate those gifts and demonstrate your skills. A dead battery doesn't do you any good, so make sure you keep your personal battery charged!

YOU OWN A SUPER MACHINE

In addition to taking care of your emotional health, another facet of self-care that I want to emphasize is physical health.

The following excerpt is from my friend, Todd Robbins, who is an expert in all things fitness, diet, and the human body. Todd has studied physical therapy and the human body his entire adult life. Todd has spent nearly 3 decades helping tens of thousands physical therapy clinics throughout the state of Pennsylvania, and over the past two decades, he has helped tens of thousands of people recover from injuries and ultimately perform at a higher level. After a recent round of golf, I asked Todd if he would contribute some to this book to help you understand how precious your health is, the amazing capabilities of your body, and why you need to keep it healthy. The following is from him:

What do you think is the most important thing you own? This answer will be different at different times of your life. At one point, I thought the most important thing I owned was a He-Man action figure toy. In high school, the most important thing I owned was my first truck, a Jeep.

The unfortunate truth is that the *things* you own can easily be taken away. Sadly, I cannot find that muscular He-Man toy or his amazing Battle Cat anymore. I cracked the engine block on that Jeep during college and haven't seen it since.

The good news is that neither my He-Man nor my Jeep are the most important things I've ever owned. *The most important thing you will ever own is your body.* It is the most amazing machine that has ever been created. The bad news is that most people know more about taking care of their cars than their bodies.

The body you have today has been developed over millenia and has been battle-tested by the forge of our terrestrial environment. It's an incredible thing. There are more neurons in your brain than stars in the known universe. Your body has more computing power than the world's most powerful computer.

Unfortunately, most people take the amazing machine they have been given for granted. It is incredibly durable and performs well, even when neglected. But many of my patients end up in my office because they don't know how important it is to maintain the physical health of their bodies. If you misuse your powerful super machine over and over, eventually it will break down, and you will need help to get back on track. However, even after years of abuse, the human body does a fantastic job of healing with the right guidance and behaviors.

Remember when you got your first car? When I first got my Jeep, I spent hours washing it, changing the oil, and doing my best to take care of it. However, as I grew older, I became a little less interested in car maintenance. After all, cars are replaceable. I knew I could always get new parts or even a new truck if I needed to. Still today, I don't pay too much attention to vehicle maintenance.

Imagine how you would treat your car if the situation was different. Let's say you were given your first car on your sixteenth birthday. You get to pick out any one you want! Pretty good deal, right? It comes with one key caveat though: it will be the only car you can own for the rest of your life. *How well would you treat that car?*

Knowing that you could never trade in that car would change how you treat it. You need it to last for the next sixty-plus years and get you where you want to go. You can replace parts, but the older your car gets, the harder it might be to do that. Also, when your car gets really old, it becomes a classic car, and the parts you'll need will be even harder to find; the mechanics qualified to fix that car will also be hard to find. If you knew you would only get one car for the rest of your life, how would it affect how well you took care of it?

When you were born, you were given the greatest gift the world has ever seen—your body. If you take care of it, it is designed to last you 110 years. Sadly, people start coming to see me when their bodies stop performing well and begin to break down. Every year the clients walking into my doors are younger. I now have patients in their forties and fifties getting new parts put into their bodies—from joints to organ replacements. That is comparable to replacing major systems in a car—like the suspension and even the engine—when the car has less than fifty thousand miles on it!

I can't teach you in so few words how to take care of the super machine you have been given; I just need to plant a seed. Endless information is available on maintaining all the systems in your body so you can keep it running well. The most important thing to understand is that your body is the only super machine you are ever going to get.

When you are younger, you feel like your body is indestructible. I know it's not easy, but I want you to look into the future and understand that you will eventually be in your twenties, your thirties, and if the universe allows, your nineties and hundreds. Once you get there, you'll have the same body you do today. Remember, life is a marathon, not a sprint. Actually, life is an ultramarathon that you should plan on running for over one hundred years. Most of my patients don't grasp the fact that they will have this same body, in some form, until it quits on them. They drive their cars as if they can trade them in for new ones. Unfortunately, the human body is much more complicated than your car.

The body you have today tells the story of what you have done with it for however many years you have been driving it. The same will be true when you are twenty, fifty, and one hundred years old. Everything you do and put into your body will result in the type of performance you get out of it. If you put good fuel, oil, and other fluids in the vehicle, it will run better. If you do the little things consistently to keep it clean and running well, *it will*. If you pay attention to the dashboard and listen to what the vehicle tells you, it will let you know when to take it in for maintenance. But if you ignore all these things, you are going to run it into the ground.

The only person who is really in charge of the maintenance of your body and how it works is you. You can get guidance from other professionals, but you are the person making the small daily decisions that result in what your body will become.

What kind of car do you want to have eighty years from now? You get to choose. Each day you are in control of making choices that will affect how that car looks and performs. Make good choices.

YOU ARE WHAT YOU EAT

Health is your greatest wealth. Most people will nod their heads in agreement when they read that, but the reality is that our daily actions typically do not correspond with that truth. Especially at your age, it is unnatural to face your mortality. Chances are, as you read this, you are healthy and strong. You have countless years ahead of you to live life to its fullest.

You can probably name a relative who lived to be close to one hundred. Through the lens of a teenager, one hundred years is an eternity. So if you gain extra weight, become out of shape, or even battle a minor sickness, in your head, you'll have plenty of time to correct it. I know this because I've had those same thoughts. It's is a battle that, frankly, I've been fighting my entire life.

This way of thinking reminds me of the expression "YOLO." If you don't know it, YOLO stands for "you only live once." (A Gen-Z or Gen Alpha equivalent might be something like, "Do it for the plot.") The general idea is that you should do whatever it is you're wanting to do, regardless of the consequences, because you only have one life to live.

YOLO encourages you to live in the moment, but it oftentimes runs headlong into your fitness-minded goals. The fitness side of you says, "Get up early, do cardio daily, lift weights, and eat healthily." The YOLO side of you says, "Skipping the workout today won't kill you; live a little. Besides, you only live once, so eat the pizza and drink the soda. You can work it off tomorrow."

But here is the deal: Every single choice you make will compound over time and determine your future. It's called the compound effect, and it's a guiding principle known by all the happiest, healthiest, wealthiest, and most successful people on the planet.

Will eating clean, healthy, fresh food today make you healthier immediately? *Not necessarily.* Or will eating fast food burgers, fries, and drinking soda make you unhealthy immediately? *Not necessarily.* As such, because we don't receive immediate results, we often don't believe our daily actions matter.

However, with every daily choice you make, you are casting a vote. Simply put, if you eat healthily, you are voting for a healthier version of you in the future. If you make poor food choices, you are voting for an unhealthier version of you in the future. But you can't see the updated results in real time. You'll get the results all at once, many months or sometimes even years down the road, when your bill of health finally comes due.

Every choice you make or don't make *matters*. It may not matter immediately, but those choices are votes, and they accumulate over time. In your future, the results of how you voted will determine the person you've physically become.

I am not an expert on physical health, but I am good at simplifying complex problems. So here are five simple tips and strategies from me to you so you can avoid reading all one million books on the market.

1. **EAT CLEAN.** Ask yourself, "Did this product come from the earth? Is it natural? Do I know what the first ingredient listed is?" Or ask, "Was this manufactured or processed in a factory? Is the first ingredient a word I may have heard in science class but have no clue what it is?" Eat clean, natural food as much as possible.

2. **DRINK WATER.** A simple rule of thumb for water consumption is to take your current body weight and divide that number in half. Now take that number and consume that many ounces of water each day. Just like all beautiful things on our planet—flowers, trees, grass, and animals—you need water and lots of it.

    Often, when you feel hungry, you are actually thirsty. Drinking water consistently throughout your days will curb your appetite. So when faced with multiple drink options, choose water as often as possible.

3. **FAST.** Your diet focuses on what you eat. Yes, that's important. But fasting focuses on when you eat, which is equally as important.

    Your body creates insulin every time you eat. Your body also uses energy to burn things in this order: sugar, then calories, then fat. If you do not eat for sixteen hours at a time—while remaining hydrated—your body creates less insulin and focuses on burning fat first.

    Assuming you sleep seven or eight hours each night, fasting for sixteen hours isn't as hard as you think. Wake up and consume water, coffee, or tea until noon. Then eat a clean lunch, consume healthy snacks, eat a clean dinner, and stop eating by 8:00 p.m. That sixteen-hour window without food from 8:00 p.m. until noon the next day will change your health forever when compounded over time.

Whichever sixteen-hour window you choose is fine. Perhaps you are more comfortable with eating between 11:00 a.m. and 7:00 p.m. or 10:00 a.m. and 6:00 p.m. You do you! Just focus on being the best possible version of yourself.

4. **AVOID PROCESSED FOOD.** The human body was not designed to eat everything you see in grocery stores, restaurants, and especially fast-food chains. This is an area many people fail as parents. Fast food is often convenient, and the fast-food chains certainly know how to make it tasty.

    However, as you enter adulthood, the choice is now yours. I challenge you to be aware of what you are putting in your body. An old cliché states, "You are what you eat." Translated, I read that as, "When you eat junk food, your body becomes junk." And conversely, "When you eat clean and healthy, your body becomes clean and healthy."

5. **CAST MORE HEALTHY VOTES THAN UNHEALTHY.** All positive choices start with awareness. Be aware that every choice you make matters when it comes to food and drinks. Read the labels, and know what you are putting into your body. Take that three-second pause to determine whether it's a vote for healthy you or unhealthy you.

Remember, with everything you do, strive for improvement, not perfection! Every once in a while, eat the cake, enjoy the donut, and drink the soda. Periodically reward yourself. The key is to consistently cast votes for *healthy you* each week.

You'll be given the opportunity to cast your vote at least ten times each day! You packed a lunch, but your friends at work want to order out. You go to a party, and there will be plenty of processed foods and sugary drinks. You know you should drink the water, but you'd just rather have something else. All day long, you will face food crossroads. It is not easy to consistently make healthy food choices. However, in the long term, it's worth it!

IT'S WHO, NOT HOW

In this chapter, I've touched on just a few of the ways to take care of yourself and keep yourself fueled for the journey ahead. I can't teach you everything, but the good news is that there are people who can. As Henry Ford said, "I don't need to know everything. I just need to know where to find it when I need it."

Your entire life, you've searched for the way to do things. While in diapers, you decided one day to make a bold move, and you attempted to crawl. Your arms gave out, and you fell on your face. Eventually, you did figure it out.

After you got sick of crawling, you pulled yourself up alongside the couch and practiced "surfing" as you stood upright and shuffled side to side while hanging on to the cushions for dear life! This led to the brave attempt to walk. Your legs gave out a few times, causing you to fall on your face. Eventually, it came to you.

When you started preschool, you likely dealt with some kind of separation anxiety, as it was the first time you spent significant hours without family nearby. But you found friends to play with in your class, and eventually, you figured it out.

Then you attempted to read words. How do they sound? What do they mean? Initially, you had no clue. You stuttered, stammered, and got a few confused along the way, but eventually, you got it.

In each of these situations and scenarios, you were never alone. As your initial crawling and first-step adventures were happening, your parents were there to pick you up. When you freaked out about being left alone at school, your teacher encouraged you into the classroom and away from Mom and Dad. When you initially struggled with reading, your teachers were patient and supportive until you learned the words and their meanings.

One of the most beautiful things about life is that you rarely have to do anything alone. Friendly faces are always nearby to help you. So ask the question, take the leap, celebrate your successes, and surround yourself with good friends. We spend too much of our time and energy seeking to answer the question, "How do I do this?" Instead, we need to ask ourselves, "Who should I do this with?" or "Who has already done this before?"

Whether it's figuring out how to master your mental, emotional, physical, or spiritual health, there are people who have been there and done that who can share the lessons they've learned along the way.

Jim Rohn once said, "You are the average of the five people you spend the most time with." In fact, I believe the greatest predictor of who you will become in the future is the people you are choosing to spend time with in the present.

Knowing *who* to surround myself rather than just knowing *how* to take care of myself has been revolutionary for the way I think about fueling myself for the journey. Ironically, it'a a lesson I learned not in the way of mental health or of physical fitness but in the business world.

I wasn't much older than you are now when I met one of my first mentors in the field of sales. His name was Lou.

Lou was one of my mother's friends who had recruited me into a multiline, home-based business. He asked me to schedule ten meetings with people so he could present our products and business opportunities. He would demonstrate the art of sales so I could learn from him and ultimately do it on my own. I called every one of my friends, and after a few days, I had ten appointments scheduled. Lou and I met with each of them, and when all the meetings were over, we had a total of zero sales. Nothing, nada, zip, zilch, zero.

Lou then gave me some advice that changed my life forever.

He said, "Scott, if you want to succeed in business or any other area of life, you have to surround yourself with people who have already done whatever it is you want to do."

If I'm being honest, those words didn't make much sense to me at the time. It wasn't until a few weeks later that I realized I was asking people my age—teenagers—to consider investing in a business opportunity that simply didn't make sense to them at that point in their life. Most had no money, were still living at home, had no business experience, and were more concerned about finding fake IDs and getting into bars than they were about building a strong financial future.

Lou challenged me to talk to people with a different vision. He asked me who the doctors, lawyers, small business owners, teachers, and other experienced leaders in the community were. He challenged me to call and schedule appointments with them.

I made a list of those people and quickly became scared to death to make calls because I assumed they wouldn't listen to a know-nothing kid asking them to explore a home-based business opportunity. Clearly, I didn't have access to the "Failure" chapter of this book at the time. I realized I was wrong quickly.

While I might have been a know-nothing kid, Lou wasn't. Lou was experienced and masterful at sales; he was everything I wanted to become. He wore nice clothes, picked up the tab at every lunch, and drove a Mercedes. Once I started scheduling appointments for community leaders to meet with Lou, my sales results exploded. I learned that, initially, I was spending too much time trying to figure out how to sell. Once I discovered whom to schedule appointments with and with whom I needed to meet, my world changed.

Focus more on *who* you surround yourself with in life and less on *how* to do things. It worked when you learned to crawl, walk, go to school, and read. I promise you it will work with everything else in your life too—whether it's keeping your personal battery charged or taking care of your super machine.

The challenge as you get older is finding the friends you need around you. The right people won't always just show up; you'll have to go out and find them. Many want to be the smartest person in the room; my challenge to you is to be the dumbest person in the room. The people you surround yourself with sharpen you into the person you're becoming, so choose who you surround yourself with wisely.

Remember, you never know how to do anything until you do. Don't waste your time uttering, "I don't know how." Instead, find somebody who does!

CHAPTER SEVEN

NO STOPPING YOU NOW

Our future is only limited by our commitment to keep the momentum going.
—ANNE SWEENEY

Imagine you're adventuring through a tropical rainforest. You were dropped in an unknown location *Man vs. Wild* style, and your goal is to make it to the nearest civilization some twenty miles away. You only have the basic tools of survival: a knife, some rope, a water canteen, and—if you're lucky—some flint and steel to make a fire.

When you first arrive, you look around and realize, *Perhaps I bit off more than I can chew.*

You look up and see striped snakes slithering through the branches of the trees above.

Yikes!

So you look down instead, and you see a Goliath beetle crawling past your foot.

Nope!

So you close your eyes—only to be inundated with the sounds of thousands of wildlife creatures teeming in the forest around you. You try to find your way through the maze of hanging vines, only to discover hours later that you're back where you started.

You ask yourself, *What was I thinking getting into this mess?*

At this point, you're at a crossroads. You can stay where you are and hope that someone will eventually come and rescue you, or you can refuse to let your fear and setbacks prevent you from reaching your goal.

Traditional wisdom would be to stay put. But you're a contrarian thinker, remember? So you decide to forge on.

You take a first step.

Then another.

Then another.

Before you know it, you've found a small stream.

Hey, those lead to rivers, and rivers lead to cities, right?

You start to feel a little better about your odds. Your confidence grows.

You make good use of the daylight hours—gaining headway, finding food, and building shelter for the night. There's not a second to waste before the sun goes down each day.

Sure, you get turned around now and then. You realize some food is harder to catch. And it takes you a couple tries to build a lean-to. But you're not letting those things get you down! It's all part of the learning curve.

By following this path, you've gained a sense of positive momentum that you know will eventually get you to your destination.

There's no stopping you now.

BEING A PERSON OF ACTION

Let's dive into how you can create the momentum that will carry you through life—from one success to the next. The first step is simple enough—and it doesn't require you to know anything. Be a person known for action.

I'm sure you've heard it said before, especially throughout your time at school, that "knowledge is power." But this old cliché only has it half right, because knowledge without action is the most-wasted resource there is for a human.

You may have the know-how to reach your goal, but if you don't take action and do something with your knowledge, what good is it? To get anywhere in life, you need to take action—no matter how small the step is or how big your fear is.

So choose to actively pursue your dreams. Waiting until the right opportunity falls into your lap won't work. It will only delay your progress and probably lead to stagnation and complacency. Instead of reaching your destination, you'll become content with whatever lot in life you were given.

By waiting passively, you'll also miss out on great chances that are available to you if you only bothered to look. As a result, you'll relinquish control of your future. You need to stand up and be the hero of your story. Any excuses you give as to why you can't take action are just that—excuses. Remember, failure is simply feedback. And feedback is your friend.

Taking action toward your goals allows you to shape your own destiny and create the opportunities you desire. When you actively pursue your dreams, you increase the likelihood of discovering opportunities you didn't know were available. The stream that leads to civilization may be just around the corner, but you'll never see it if you don't bother to look. Your proactive efforts can open doors that waiting around never would.

In my own life, once I started studying business and entrepreneurship, I began to believe that life was possible for me. I could be an entrepreneur too. After a certain point of working for corporate America, I reached a crossroad: I could take action, better myself, and just go for it—*or* I could keep working for someone else and watch others do it.

Personally, entrepreneurship was the dream. And while I didn't know if I would fail, I knew it was what I wanted and that, if I didn't take action, I'd be stuck in a cycle of working for someone else while merely dreaming about doing something that was important to me. I had to dive in and take action, or it would never happen.

Even if I had faced setbacks that forced me to give up my goal, it still would have been worth trying, and I would have been grateful for the feedback from the failure.

But I didn't fail. I took action, became an entrepreneur, and found many amazing opportunities along the way that I never would have had the chance to enjoy if I had passively sat back and waited for my life to just unfold before me.

No matter what your dream is—entrepreneurship or employed work, creating or serving—you need to take action, one step at a time, in order to achieve it. Taking action can look different for everyone, but there are a few basic steps you can take to significantly reduce your resistance.

Stop giving excuses as to why you can't do something, and don't wait until "later." Procrastination sounds pretty tempting at the moment, but in the long run, it isn't a helpful tool for achieving your dreams. Act now, and get the ball rolling.

Don't wait to feel totally confident or totally knowledgeable before you begin. Confidence and knowledge come *from* experience. Start with action, and the rest will follow.

Sharpen your saw, then go cut some trees. In other words, refine your skills, then put them to use in achieving the life you want. The best way to learn is by getting dirty and making mistakes.

When you take action, the life you want to live is closer than you think. So what action have you been putting off? Put your dreams in motion by taking that action today. Don't wait to become your own action hero.

CULTIVATING CONFIDENCE

To maintain the momentum wave that carries you from one success to the next, confidence is key. It's estimated that roughly 85 percent of people worldwide have low self-confidence. We doubt our ability to do our jobs, our intelligence, our looks, and even our likability.

And that lack of confidence affects us both personally and professionally. In fact, research has found that those who have confidence make considerably more in their jobs. In the blue-collar sector, those with confidence make about $7,000 more annually than those who lack it. In the white-collar sector, that number jumps to $28,000 more annually.

The good news is that if confidence is something you lack, it's a skill you can build. Confidence isn't learned; it's earned. As you take action, your confidence grows.

A great example of this is learning how to ride a bike. When you're just starting out as a four- or five-year-old, learning how to ride a two-wheel pedal bike is one of the scariest things you can do. You know you're bound to crash at some point before you figure it out. So you prefer the training wheels or a parent holding on to you.

But when the safety net of your parents or training wheels is removed, it's up to you to figure it out. When Dad lets go, you have to keep pedaling. After a few pedals, you realize you're still up. You realize, *I can do this!* And before you know it, you're doing it! You're balancing the bike and zooming around without any fear. Your physical momentum literally grew as a result of your newfound confidence. By the end of summer, you're riding with no hands and trying other tricks around the neighborhood.

If you weren't willing to try things and fail, you'd still be crawling. But you're walking now. You failed and fell down countless times, but you got back up, took action, and tried again. This proves that you have figured things out in the past, and you did so by *doing*. Once you began taking those steps on your own, you gained confidence, slowly learning how to jog, run, and jump.

And just like when you learned to ride a bike, you didn't grow your confidence by reading a book. You learned as you *practiced*. After each wipeout, you figured out what not to do. As you got better, you became more comfortable, which built your confidence. And with that confidence, you pushed the limits, tried new things, and developed new skills.

The key to gaining that confidence is just going for it. You pedal, learn as you go, and see yourself improve each time. Seeing the incremental growth makes you feel better about yourself, and you begin to perform better as a result. Your momentum builds.

This same cycle applies to anything in life. By taking action, you build confidence for whatever you're doing. And that confidence improves your performance and success, giving you the courage to take more action.

Confident people are more likely to set ambitious goals and pursue them with determination. They believe in their ability to succeed and are motivated to put in the necessary effort. It's this drive that leads to higher levels of achievement and personal fulfillment.

Building confidence is a gradual process. To do so, you must take proactive steps to change your mindset and learn new skills. Start with small, manageable goals, and gradually work your way up to bigger challenges. Achieving these goals will give you a sense of accomplishment and boost your confidence. Identify your strengths and talents, and celebrate your achievements. Step out of your comfort zone, and tackle your fears head-on. Your confidence will grow each time you face and overcome a fear.

Gradually building and maintaining a higher level of confidence will enable you to face challenges and pursue your goals with greater self-assurance. So don't wait to feel ready to do something. You'll be waiting for a long time if so. Instead, take action! Go after what you want, and confidence will follow.

THE VALUE OF TIME

What is your most valuable resource? Instinctively, you might think it's money, skills, or health. But while those are valuable in their own right, they aren't your most valuable resource. *Time is.*

Unlike most other resources which you can get more of, your time is finite. Once you use it all up, you'll never get it back again. You can regain lost money, acquire new skills, or recover physical health, but you can't recover lost time.

That's why it's paramount that you steward your time well. Otherwise, you'll miss your chance to build and keep the momentum you want in your life.

Many people have their sights set on accumulating money and forget that their time is limited. Often they believe that they'll be able to enjoy their lives once they have enough money—only to get to the end of their lives and realize that they treated their money as more valuable than their time.

Don't misorder your priorities and wait to do what matters most to you until the end of your life. Be strategic and intentional with how you structure your days and how you choose to spend your time. When you're young, it may seem like you have lots of time to burn. You think you have an unlimited supply and don't have to worry about it as much. But making the best of your time starting at a young age can propel you much further in life.

Everything you do comes at the expense of something else. There's always a cost or trade-off with how you spend your time. But the choice is up to you. I want to encourage you to fully immerse yourself in the present. Whatever you are doing, do it. Avoid distractions, or risk missing out on the greatest gift you are ever given at this very moment.

Now, many people think they can get the most out of their time by multitasking. But that's a myth. You can't effectively and efficiently do two things at once. Do whatever is the primary thing you should be doing at this moment, then move on to the next. This is why setting goals and casting a vision are important. These things help you understand and prioritize what you want to do with your time. Make a choice of how you'll spend your time, then do just that. Prioritizing your goals is what's most important. Don't try to do everything at once.

Every day has plenty of time so long as you only focus on a few essential items. Determine what your priorities are for that specific day, then make sure you accomplish them first so that your day is successful.

Here's how to make sure you're spending your time efficiently and effectively:

First, either before you go to bed or first thing in the morning, make a list of everything you want to get done in the day to come. Let it flow freely out of you for several minutes so you can capture everything on paper.

Then designate your priorities. Ask yourself what the one thing is that you need to accomplish in order to feel good about your day. Put a "#1" by that task. What is the second thing you need to get done? Put a "#2" by it. Then do it a third time.

Once you have two or three tasks marked, your to-do list is now an "Essentials" list—and you know exactly what you need to do that day. With this clarity, you can give laserlike focus to your priorities in the order that you marked them. Once you finish number 1, move on to number 2, and so on. If you keep going down the list past the two or three you've marked, that's amazing. Keep the momentum going.

When the day is over, everything you didn't get done gets pushed to the next day. As you sit down to make your list again, add any additional tasks that have come up, and repeat the process of selecting your top two or three priorities to get done. If you find yourself repeatedly avoiding a certain task for multiple days in a row, that may be a sign it's not truly a priority for you. Fill your time with what is important, and repeat this process every work day.

This is a process I've been following for years, and it has changed my life. It's forced me to delegate, outsource, or say "no" to all the nonessential things and hone in with laser focus on my priorities to make sure I'm moving the ball down the field every single day.

Time waits for no one. It just keeps going, whether you are ready or not—with or without you. Tomorrow you will wake up one day older and one day closer to the end of your time on earth. Will you spend your time on the things that are important to you, or will you squander it?

The biggest thing to be aware of with time is that everything positive or negative in your life is the result of doing something or not doing something over a long period. Any lasting success is going to take time. Nothing happens quickly. Success requires putting in the work—whether that be investing your money, practicing physical fitness, or going to college and earning a degree. Since it will take time to get to your end goal, it's vital that you start today.

Sit down tonight and make your "Essentials" list for tomorrow. Determine what you will focus on first thing tomorrow, then get it done when the morning comes. Get rid of the excuses, and move yourself toward your goals. As you do, you're keeping the ball rolling and your momentum building.

CONTINUAL LEARNING

If your goal is to find your way out of the jungle and to your destination, you have to be ready and willing to learn. To build and keep momentum, continual learning, both personally and professionally, is vital.

In school, you were told which subjects you would study and what you needed to learn. But now you get to choose your own adventure. You should always be looking to learn, but you're at the steering wheel when it comes to which direction you want to take it.

I truly believe this is the greatest time in the history of our world to be your age, especially when it comes to learning. When I got out of college, there were no podcasts, TED Talks, or YouTube. If I wanted to see a Tony Robbins talk, I had to pay $10,000—and I didn't have $10!

But you have access to all the greatest talks ever—from Tony Robbins to the titans of industries. There's a wealth of information available to you for free anytime you want or need it. The whole world is yours to explore. You don't need permission to ditch a book that isn't of interest or not pursue a program that isn't fulfilling to you. Why waste your time on things that are of no interest to you? Instead, you get to focus on the material that lights you up and creates a hunger in you for more.

When I was in school, I wasn't a great student because nothing was of interest to me. I might have read two books total in high school, and that was because I had to. When I felt no connection to the content, it was like pulling teeth getting me to read. But when I got into the business world and started learning how to become an entrepreneur, I couldn't get enough. I began learning about sales and the psychology behind it, diving deep into topics that interested me. Now I can't stop buying books on these topics!

You might be like me back then. When you hear "continuous learning," you might be tempted to think, "No way! I put in my time learning, and now I'm done."

But the kind of learning you'll do now is nothing like what you did in school. Any learning you do now will be about what interests you, and you get the awesome opportunity to learn from the greatest people who have ever done these things.

Continuous learning is incredibly important throughout life because it promotes both personal and professional growth and development. It keeps your skills relevant, enhances adaptability, and fosters innovation—all of which keep your momentum going.

What do you want to learn about? What interests you, excites you, and makes you want to know more? These are the passions you want to explore and develop a greater understanding of. Let loose, and follow your curiosity to see where it leads. Follow what interests you, and allow those passions to grow through continuous learning.

Without continuous learning, people tend to develop a fixed mindset. They believe that their abilities and talents cannot be changed or have reached their peak. They wrongly think that any effort in an area where they're not naturally talented is a waste of time. They quit trying, quit learning, and as a result, quit being successful.

But those who make learning a priority develop a growth mindset and the ability to adapt when setbacks arise. These people believe their abilities and intelligence can be developed through learning and hard work, so they focus on acquiring knowledge.

This knowledge empowers them to acquire new skills that keep them competitive for new career opportunities and sharpens their mental agility, helping them process information and make decisions more effectively. As a result, their success continues to grow, and they are propelled forward.

Developing the habit of continuous learning isn't difficult to do. You just need to actively seek out knowledge and challenges that push your boundaries and help you grow. So stay curious, read widely, and join communities that prize continuous learning.

Sustained effort is key to mastering new skills and achieving long-term goals. If you set aside a dedicated time each day for learning, you are sure to maximize your growth potential, so start today!

Commit ten to fifteen minutes a day to reading or learning something new. Block that time on your calendar now. That way you'll look back at yourself from five years ago and shake your head at how little you knew then.

LIFE ISN'T LINEAR

As you strive to build and keep momentum in life, my last piece of advice is to remember that life isn't linear. It doesn't follow a straightforward, predictable path. Instead, it's full of unexpected twists, turns, setbacks, and breakthroughs. This concept challenges the conventional belief that life should progress in a smooth, orderly manner—like moving from one stage to the next without deviation.

It's easy to believe the path should be straightforward. You go to school, get good grades, move to higher education, get a good job, work hard, get a better job or raise, meet your life partner, retire with lots of money, and live happily ever after.

But in reality, life is unpredictable and complex. And it is full of surprises—both good and bad. Unexpected events like losing a job, discovering a new passion, or meeting someone who changes your path can disrupt any planned course of action.

Oftentimes the surprises will be good things! As you learn more about yourself and the world, your goals, desires, and values can shift. What you wanted at one point in life might no longer satisfy you later. And that realization frees you to pursue new passions.

But negative changes are inevitable parts of life too. Though you will have failures and setbacks, these don't signal the end of your journey, just the conclusion of that specific journey. In fact, setbacks can often lead to greater resilience and new opportunities.

Regardless of whether you initially view a change as good or bad, keep in mind that there are always multiple paths to success. If you buy the idea that there's only one path, any deviation may seem like a roadblock to your momentum. But just like Yogi Berra's advice about forks in the road, there's often more than one way to reach your destination. You might take a different path than expected and still end up where you want to be—or somewhere even better.

In 2021, I was having an "identity crisis." I owned multiple thriving businesses, and I was financially secure. But I didn't feel confident I was pursuing work that was meaningful to me. I wasn't personally spending my time focused on activities that lit me up.

In an effort to rebuild my personal momentum, I made a commitment to be continually learning. I focused on personal and professional development by reading high-quality books and listening to podcasts. This led me to connect with and be coached by a business leader who helped others build their personal brands.

Through my coaching sessions and daily journaling, I realized I was best suited to serve the person I once was: a confused teenager lacking confidence and direction. My brand strategist encouraged me to lean into this calling and dive deeper into this work. They introduced me to a book publishing company, and now you are reading *these pages* as a result.

Three years prior, I was the owner of an insurance agency and a business coach to entrepreneurs. I never would have imagined I'd now be working with young adults, helping them transition into their career after the classroom. But here we are—because life is not linear.

The tension between the idealized version of life and the messy reality is a common challenge that many people face. We often grow up with a vision of how life "should" unfold—a series of neatly ordered milestones. However, reality tends to be much messier, full of unexpected detours, failures, and surprises that can make us question the validity of our dreams.

The idealized version of life is built on expectations—often influenced by societal norms, media portrayals, opinions of family, and personal aspirations. This version is usually linear, predictable, and filled with success at every step. It's a vision where things go according to plan, where hard work always pays off, and where setbacks are rare or easily overcome. It's stable and secure with minimal disruptions. Once you achieve something, it remains constant.

In contrast, the messy reality of life is far from predictable. Life is full of uncertainties, and things don't often go as planned. You don't find success at every step, setbacks are common, and instability is the status quo.

Reconciling the tension between dreams and reality involves a shift in perspective. To make that shift, it's necessary to accept that life's unpredictability doesn't invalidate your dreams but rather enriches your journey toward them.

The first step is to adjust and manage your expectations. Life's unpredictability means that sometimes things won't go as you'd hoped. Adjusting your expectations to include the possibility of change and challenge can reduce the disappointment when reality doesn't match the ideal.

Second, be willing to embrace flexibility. Your path may not be straightforward, and that's okay. Being flexible with your plans allows you to adapt to changes and still work toward your goals. Just as life isn't linear, your approach to achieving your dreams doesn't have to be rigid.

Third, cultivate resilience. This will help you bounce back from setbacks and continue moving forward. Resilience is developed by facing challenges head-on, learning from them, and maintaining a positive outlook, even when things get tough. As Dr. Martin Luther King Jr. once said, "The ultimate measure of a man is not where he stands in moments of comfort and convenience, but where he stands at times of challenge and controversy."

Finally, focus on the journey, not just the destination. The messy reality of life teaches you that the journey is as important as the destination. The experiences you gather, the resilience you build, and the wisdom you gain along the way are invaluable. By focusing on these, you'll be better positioned to roll with the punches.

The gap between the idealized version of life and the messy reality can be a source of frustration and disillusionment. However, by adjusting your goals, embracing flexibility, cultivating resilience, and focusing on the journey, you can navigate this tension more effectively.

Life's unpredictability doesn't mean you should abandon your dreams. Instead, it should invite you to approach them with a mindset that is open to growth, change, and the unexpected twists and turns that make life truly rich and meaningful. When you do, you'll be able to keep your momentum despite anything life throws at you.

CHAPTER EIGHT

SEEDING THE PATH

The best time to plant a tree is twenty years ago. The second best time is today.
—ANCIENT CHINESE PROVERB

As you've learned, *life isn't linear*. It's full of winding turns, twists, and loops. You may think you're headed in a totally new direction, but oftentimes, you'll find yourself back in a place you stood before, and you'll relearn lessons that you thought you've already walked through.

But that doesn't mean you're doing something wrong. Retracing your steps is a part of life—and it can actually be a good thing. In Egyptian Arabic, the word *human* means "to forget." That just shows that it's part of our nature to forget lessons we think we've learned and to have to come back to them again and again.

Since this path is one you're likely to return to, trust me when I say, it's well worth your time to plant some seeds along the way.

By taking these little steps now, you're giving a gift to Future You, who will benefit from the harvest of what you've planted.

In this chapter, we'll dive into how to plant these seeds by implementing some beneficial and enduring habits and customs. You may not witness the immediate results, but I can assure you, somewhere down the road, you'll find that you reap what you sow.

THE LUCKY BAMBOO TREE

Allow me to introduce you to two teenagers. One is named Eddie Excuses, and the other is Successful Sally. Eddie and Sally typically choose different directions at the crossroads of their lives.

For instance, Eddie and Sally once met a wealthy and powerful emperor, who gave both of them the secret to his success. Simply put, the emperor told them to plant the seeds of a bamboo tree and then continuously water them until they grow. He explained that the only way to fail would be to stop watering those seeds.

On the surface, this seemed easy enough. Both Eddie and Sally planted the bamboo tree seeds. Then, each day, they made sure the soil was watered and fertilized morning, afternoon, and night. Day after day, they nurtured the soil and created an ideal growing environment.

After a week, the soil looked exactly the same as it did on day one. In fact, it looked exactly the same after a month. They each thought this was crazy. Every single day, three times a day, they watered their patches of dirt, and absolutely nothing happened. However, they trusted this leader, who shared what he called "life-changing advice" with them. Why would he lie?

One month turned into two, and two months turned into three. Still nothing. Eddie's and Sally's friends would pass by, asking them what they were up to. After explaining they were watering their bamboo trees, their friends laughed.

One sarcastically said, "Those aren't trees. They are patches of dirt, no different than three months ago."

That friend wasn't wrong.

It was then that Eddie allowed self-doubt to enter his brain.

What if the seeds I planted were no good?
What if the soil is bad?
What if the temperatures aren't right?
What if the emperor was wrong?
How many more days am I going to waste time watering and fertilizing this patch of dirt and getting laughed at with no results?

The answer was zero. Eddie was done wasting his time on this project. He tried, and it didn't work. He had a solid list of excuses for why it was no longer worth his time and effort.

But Sally chose to press on. Months turned into a year, and one year turned into two. Two full years of getting up each morning to water a patch of soil with nothing to show for it—not even a little green sprout.

Self-doubt crept into Sally's mind the same way it did with Eddie. Her friends continued laughing at her, and some even questioned her sanity, but she refused to quit. Each time quitting entered her mind, she refocused on the successful leader, who shared stories of how his life and the lives of so many other successful friends had changed forever once their bamboo trees grew. He had warned Eddie and Sally that it wouldn't be a quick and easy process, but he encouraged them to have *faith* and promised their efforts would be rewarded. So Sally pressed on.

Two years turned into three, and then three years turned into four. Still, there was no sign of a bamboo tree.

And then it happened. One magical moment, while watering her patch of soil for the four thousandth time, a bright-green sprout emerged from the earth and grew six inches tall.

Sally was elated! Her hard work and perseverance were finally going to pay off. The next morning, that sprout grew another two feet with new sprouts growing from it. The next day, the baby bamboo tree was taller than Sally. And before she knew it, four weeks had passed, and her bamboo tree had grown to over eighty feet tall! It now stood the same height as a four-story building.

Suddenly, everything in Sally's life changed, just like the emperor had promised her four years earlier. Sally's happiness increased, her wealth expanded, and her opportunities became abundant. Her friends started to call it her lucky bamboo tree.

Was it actually *luck* though? Or was it the result of four years of dedication, focused work, and commitment to a single goal?

And did that tree really grow eighty feet in four weeks? Or did it grow underneath the soil that Sally was watering every day for four years straight?

Circling back to a lesson from earlier in this book, Sally had planted the seeds of *faith* and *grit*, which carried her to her eventual success. If you recall, *faith* is complete trust and belief in something or somebody. And *grit* is the dedicated action required to continuously follow your *faith*—even though you cannot see the results. Just like Sally, those two words will change the direction of your life forever if you choose.

Four years earlier, Eddie and Sally began watering the soil, and they both had faith that a bamboo tree would grow. What they didn't know at the time was that from the moment those first drops of water hit their seeds, the bamboo trees began to grow underground.

As they continued to water and fertilize the soil, a root system expanded and grew stronger beneath the surface. It was building the rock-solid foundation required to one day explode from the earth and support an eighty-foot tree.

They both started with faith, but grit was required to show up every morning to care for that soil. When Eddie's grit stopped, so too did his faith that something good would happen. On that day, his lucky bamboo tree died.

Like Sally, when you truly believe in something with all of your heart, pursue that passion and protect your strong beliefs from naysayers. Not everyone will see, believe, or understand your vision, and that's okay. In fact, that's what makes it *your* vision.

There is no such thing as overnight success. The actress, singer, or athlete who just hit the mainstream and is suddenly making millions of dollars didn't just start putting in the work recently. You just happen to see the results of their work now. They put in years of faith and grit to earn what they are receiving. It wasn't luck. It never is.

Hold on to this truth: anything worth having is worth working for. Throughout your life's journey, you will pursue many passions. Along the way, you will arrive at some of the most challenging crossroads. Your can either fight through the failures and push through the pain of not realizing results, or you can surrender to that voice in your head telling you to stop. Never surrender. Have faith, and work with grit.

OTHERS AHEAD OF SELF

Mother Teresa once said, "The greatest good is what we do for one another." Surround yourself with people willing to trade one of their biggest moments for you. Likewise, be willing to do the same. Just like faith and grit, putting others before yourself is another seed you plant that will serve you well in the long run.

Growing up in Central New York, I always rooted for the Syracuse University football team. Some of my most special childhood moments came from attending games at their home field, which was named the Carrier Dome at the time.

As a child, I dreamed of being able to play on the football field inside the Dome. As my athletic career progressed, it became pretty obvious by my freshman year of high school that if I was going to play on that field, it wouldn't be as a Syracuse University athlete.

Though my football skills weren't Syracuse-level, I had a unique opportunity to play in the Dome in high school since it was the venue for our local sectional championship games.

To add to that, I got to play with some exceptional friends. Travis Robbins and his twin brother, Todd, were exceptional athletes and have always been exceptional humans. They were in the grade below me, but we always played sports together growing up. Life sometimes blesses us with "brothers from another mother." And the Robbins twins were that to me.

On the high school football team, I was the left-side cornerback, and my jersey was number 3. Travis was the left outside linebacker, and his jersey was number 10. Before every play, we communicated with one another after reading the offense's alignment. We defended passes together, gang-tackled together, teased each other when somebody messed up, bled together, sweat together, pushed one another during wind sprints, and weight-trained during the off-season.

For three years, we had one common goal: to win a sectional championship on the football field at the Dome. Everything was set up for us to do just that heading into my senior year (Travis's junior year). We had a solid season the previous year and were returning all but a handful of starters. Our team was favored to win it all!

The season started exactly as planned. We were 5–0 out of the gate and ready to knock off our division rivals to go 6–0. After that two very beatable teams were on the schedule, and it would be off to the Dome to fulfill our childhood dream.

Everything was going great during that sixth game. We were up 23–7 at halftime. We got the ball to start the third quarter, marched down the field, made it to the one-yard line, and were poised to go up 30–7 and put the game away.

But here's a not-so-fun fact about life: sometimes, when everything seems to be going great, suddenly *everything crashes on top of you.*

We turned the ball over in the end zone on that play from the one-yard line. The other team responded by scoring a touchdown on their next possession, another after that, another after that, and yet another after that.

The final score was 40–23. We lost. I was crushed. In fact, I cried. I sat at my locker in full pads, head in my hands, just numb for thirty minutes. I couldn't move, didn't want to move, and didn't want to do anything. Everything we had worked so hard to achieve for several years was now over in an instant. *The dream of my maroon and white number 3 Grates jersey playing on that Dome turf was truly dead.*

To this day, three decades later, I still get emotional thinking about that game and what could have been. And while countless life lessons occurred through this adversity, the biggest lesson came from my good friend, Travis Robbins.

Fast-forward one year.

I was playing Division 3 football at St. John Fisher College as a freshman. As seniors, Todd and Travis Robbins were now co-captains of the high school football team. They had the opportunity to finish what we had started, and they did!

After an incredible regular season, the team made it to the sectional finals to be played at the Carrier Dome. Obviously, I would be there to root my brothers on. I knew it would be emotional watching them compete on that field without me, but I had no idea how emotional it would be.

The night before the game, Travis called me and said, "I have a special surprise for you tomorrow." Those words were part of a much longer conversation and didn't strike me at the time. His surprise did strike me when the team took the field though. After working his entire childhood to play that one game at the Dome, Travis finally got to run onto the field for the first time.

But he wasn't wearing his number 10 jersey. Instead, Travis got ahold of *my* number 3 jersey. He wore it and played his heart out that game as if I were there with him. He had taken one of the biggest moments of his life and shared it with me.

You've already learned that, in life, you'll find plenty of *energy vampires*. These are people who will suck the life right out of you. They will take things from you, spread negativity, point fingers, and find fault in everything and everyone except themselves.

You'll also find a rare breed of people who constantly put others ahead of themselves. That was Travis.

One of my favorite mantras is this: *Those who always give will always have.* My friend Travis gave me something special that day. That memory didn't cost him a dime, but it will last me a lifetime.

My challenge to you is to avoid the energy vampires, find friends like Travis, and most importantly, *be the person always seeking opportunities to improve the lives of others.* The secret to living is giving.

At several moments in life, you will have the choice to do something special for or by yourself, but you'll also have the opportunity to give that something special or share that something special with somebody else. When you arrive at such a crossroads, do what Travis Robbins did: put others ahead of yourself.

When you do, you're giving your friends memories that will last, and you're investing in the vital, enduring relationships that will help hold you up during your rough patches in life.

Life is filled with *peaks* and *valleys*. When you surround yourself with people who put your needs ahead of theirs and you reciprocate their goodwill, you'll enjoy the peaks more as you celebrate with those who cheer you on, and you'll make it through the valleys because you won't be doing it alone.

UNCONDITIONAL LOVE

To foster the kind of relationships that will last you a lifetime, you have to root them in unconditional love. In the words of Stephen Kendrick, "The only way love can last a lifetime is if it's unconditional. The truth is this: Love is not determined by the one being loved, but rather the one choosing to love."

To give your love unconditionally is to do so without expecting anything in return. It's easy to utter "I love you" and mean it on a surface level but not in its deepest form. To love another human unconditionally is to have the ability to say "I love you" and mean it with your whole heart without the expectation of anything in return.

I truly love my family unconditionally. But I admit it's not easy to give all of yourself to another human, expecting nothing in return. In fact, it's the scariest thing in the world to do.

For me, I'm empowered to love my family unconditionally as a result of my faith in God. When nothing makes sense or seems to be going right, your faith that will lead, guide, and comfort you.

At the same time, my family encourages me to love unconditionally because I know they love me that way too. Whenever things in your life are scary, confusing, unfair, or illogical, it's your family who you will turn to. These people love you unconditionally. They don't just say it; they mean it. When it's time to turn words into reality, these people will trade their lives to save yours.

For some, family means blood relatives. For others, while they aren't related by blood, they share a family bond that is just as strong. Ultimately, any other person whom you choose to love unconditionally is your family.

How do you know when you love someone or when someone loves you at this level? Well, let's take a look at emperor penguins and how deeply they love.

A male emperor penguin will march continually, day and night, for over seventy miles—which isn't easy with those tiny legs—to find his soulmate. We think it's cute when we see a penguin sliding on its belly, but in reality, they are doing so because their little legs are exhausted and need a rest from the march.

Once the male emperor penguin finds a female emperor penguin to love unconditionally, the female penguin lays an egg and then leaves for the water to feed. Now it's up to the male penguin to balance the egg on his feet, resting his body above the egg to keep it warm. Should the emperor penguin wobble and uncover this egg for any extended period of time, it will freeze.

Remember, these penguins are in Antarctica on a giant open glacier. There's no shelter, the temperatures are below zero, and the winds can gust over one hundred miles per hour. How long does the male emperor penguin warm this egg, protecting it from these extreme conditions? *Two months!*

As if the freezing, windy conditions weren't enough, the male emperor penguin starves for over 120 days to care for this egg and then the newly hatched baby penguin until its mother returns. When the mother does return, she meets their new child, and the father leaves to feed on fish. Once full, he returns, and the family is officially reunited.

When it comes to family, commitment, and love, I challenge you to be like a penguin.

You will be a part of numerous groups throughout your life. I like to call them tribes. You'll have different tribes of friends, coworkers, sports teams, and many others. The names and faces will change within all those tribes. People will enter and exit your life throughout the various seasons. However, the only eternal tribe you'll be a part of is *your family.*

Care for, protect, and love your family deeper than all others in your life. It's not always easy to do. But nothing in life is. Because your love for family is so great and you *give* it unconditionally, your expectations for your family may oftentimes be higher. These high expectations can lead to disappointment when family members fall short of your hopes. Hesitate to be critical, and focus on being helpful during times like these.

You'll find plenty of moments in your future when a family member will disappoint you. Understand that the greater you love somebody, the greater this pain feels when they fall short of your expectations. You'll always have two options: You can *forgive*, or you can allow those negative feelings to fester. For your own sake and the sake of the relationship, always choose the path of forgiveness.

It's easy to take a family member's love for granted. We assume our bond is so tight that we don't always need to actively love and support one another. However, this isn't true.

Understand the law of familiarity—which states that when you get exposed to a certain person, place, or thing for enough time, you'll become familiar with it. When you become familiar with it, your appreciation for it dies down. In other words, you start taking it for granted.

Choose to be there for your family. Often you can make a quick call, send a text message, or drop by for a visit with a family member. Whenever possible, make the time for conversations and quality time. The topic of conversation doesn't matter. The simple act of communicating lets your family members know you care, and that means the world to them.

Almost everything in life is temporary, including our actual lives themselves. A family bond is the closest thing we have to permanent. Care for those relationships above all others. Always be there for family—just like the emperor penguin who cares for his egg. When we lose sight of the importance of maintaining a loving relationship with those who love us most, it's like waddling away from that egg and exposing it to harsh, freezing conditions.

Unconditional love can be hard, but it is the deepest, most meaningful form of love. It's the glue that forms the bonds that last—and you can't keep enduring ties without it. Allow yourself to care for another human at this level. It's equal parts scary and exhilarating. But I can promise you that Future You will thank you for it.

TRADITIONS

When I was born, my grandparents owned a basset hound named Willy. Basset hounds are the cutest little ugly dogs. They have short legs, stay low to the ground, have long ears that they almost trip over while walking, and have very loving but droopy eyes.

While shopping for my first Christmas, my mother found a gift box with a basset hound that looked just like Willy on the box. One of the first presents I ever opened was inside the "Willy box." From that year on, it became a tradition that the last gift I would open was the one wrapped inside that box.

Through the years, the box aged, just like we do. As it became older, it had rips and tears. By the time I reached my teen years, the box could no longer be wrapped using paper or tape. When I reached high school, the box itself became the gift my mother gave me.

The Willy box was a family tradition that strengthened the bond between my mother and me. I honestly couldn't name a single gift that was ever inside it, but each year it was that gift I was most excited to receive. Looking back, I now realize my excitement wasn't created by the gift or even the box, but rather *the tradition* and knowing that I received another year to celebrate Christmas with my mother.

Family traditions are recreated year after year and become events you look forward to. These traditions provide comfort and security.

Each year our lives change as we all go through different seasons. Some of these changes are great, but others aren't. In some seasons, we soak in the sun; in others, we shiver in the cold. But through it all, these family traditions give us hope and generate anticipation of something exciting. They provide stability in a world that never stops moving.

Because the holidays are on the calendar each year, it's easy to create family traditions around those dates—and that's great! However, family traditions can take place whenever you choose.

As I reflect on my parenting days, I remember doing weeklong camping trips with another family each summer, hiking up a mountain each fall, and going on our boys' baseball trip to a different major league stadium every spring.

Some of our greatest memories are created by family traditions. These traditions force us to make time for specific events and enjoy the moments we have with one another. When a family member's time here on earth ends, these traditions help us remember them and keep their spirit alive.

When it comes to traditions, it can be easy to compare one year to the next and ramp up expectations. Keep in mind that people change, the weather changes, and every new day is unique from the one that came before it—and that's okay. Treat each year within a tradition as what it is: a brand-new event surrounded by a new set of circumstances. The differences will be what ultimately make the memory.

As you leave the classroom and gear up for the next season of your life, I encourage you to maintain some special traditions and start some new ones as well. Take something that you are passionate about—something you truly enjoy doing—and find a way to involve others in it each year.

As you do, you'll find that these will become some of the memories you'll cherish the longest—and things you'll look forward to most each year. As Gustav Mahler put it, "Tradition is not the worship of ashes, but the preservation of fire."

Life gets busy, and you will consistently utter the words, "I don't have enough time." You will find yourself pulled in numerous directions with your own career, family, and hobbies. At times you won't want to attend or help plan an upcoming family tradition.

When this happens, I encourage you to reflect on all the great memories you have from past family gatherings and ask yourself what life would be like without them. Choose to make the time. Everything else can wait.

LEGACY

The final seed I'd encourage you to plant for the future is legacy. When you're no longer on this earth, how will you be remembered, and what will you leave behind?

If you and a friend were going to head out on an adventure to a place you've never visited before, what's one of the first things you'd do when you get into the car?

You'd enter the address of your destination into your Maps app, right? That way you'd know exactly where you are heading step by step. If you didn't put in your destination, that journey would be *much* different. Essentially, you'd be playing a guessing game—and burning through your gas tank as you do it.

Our lives are no different. You can have whatever life you want, but you first have to type your final destination into your map.

I want to challenge you to spend some time thinking about the one thing nobody wants to think about: death. Imagine a date at least seventy years into the future. As you do, think about what it would be like to read your own obituary. When your final day comes, what will be written about you to summarize your life?

Weird, right? I know from personal experience. In my freshman year of college, a professor assigned us the task of writing out our own obituary, and now I assign it to you.

Writing your own obituary as a young adult is a form of goal-setting and an efficient way to define your vision. Essentially, you are typing your final destination into the map app of your life. I encourage you to put some deep thought into this. Use these questions as a guide, and summarize your anticipated life in five hundred words or less.

- What names will be listed as people who loved you the most?
- What level of education did you achieve?
- What type of career did you have?
- What were your hobbies?
- What were you most passionate about?
- Ultimately, what *impact* did you make during your time here?

People will often tell you that *life is short*. Even if we live to be 150, that's not a long time in the grand scheme of things. The only parts of our lives that can last forever are our legacies. Simply put, our legacy is how we are remembered and what we are remembered for after our obituaries are written.

Once you know what you want your legacy to be, then you can spend all your living years making it come true. Think of a deceased person who made a difference in your life, who still inspires you, or who you think about often. To you that person is a legend. And legacies of legends never die.

Keep in mind that your legacy is not dictated by that of your family who came before. You have the ability to alter the direction of your family for generations to come—to be the person whose branch stands out on the family tree. Don't allow other family members' journeys—past or present—to determine your path. Don't allow your family's identity—good or bad—to dictate your life. Only you get to write the story of your life. You have every right and all the ability to be the one person in the family who changes the tree. What an amazing opportunity!

I'll end with this:

One of my favorite books of all time is *The Slight Edge* by Jeff Olson. One of my biggest takeaways from his book is a section where he talks about funerals. Jeff says that at the average funeral, only about *ten people* cry. He asks, "You mean I go through my entire life, spend years enduring all those trials and tribulations and achievements and joys and heartbreaks—and at the end of it there are only ten people in the world who care enough to show up and cry?"

What's more, Jeff reports that, after the few tears are shed, the top factor that would determine how many people would go on from the funeral to attend the actual burial would be *the weather*. He says, "If it happened to be raining, 50% of the people who attended my funeral would decide maybe they wouldn't go on to attend my burial after all and just head home."

When I read this, I couldn't believe it. However, it did put things into perspective for me. Suddenly, I flashed back to teenage me sitting in the college library during freshman year, working on my own obituary, and I realized where I should focus my legacy.

Who helped me most from the moment of my birth? *My family.* Who helped create all those wonderful memories I have around traditions? *My family.* Who were the first people I mentioned while writing my own obituary? *My family.* Who would be the ten people who cried at my funeral and stand by my graveside in the rain when all is said and done? *My family.*

So why am I spending so much time trying to please and impress everyone else? You have the power to write the story of your life. But keep in mind that the main characters—and the people who will actually feel the effects of your legacy—will always be your family.

As you plant the seeds of your legacy, you won't always get it right. The cool thing about your Maps app is that when it tells you to turn right, but you turn left instead, it simply recalculates and puts you back on the right path to get you to wherever you want to go.

Life works like that too. Just because you took a wrong turn doesn't mean you can't get back on the right track. You have your goals and your vision board. You now know how you want your obituary to read and what you want your legacy to be. You're going to be intentional with your decisions to make it all happen. So when you make wrong turns along the way, don't stress. Instead, trust the map you created, and recalculate to get back on track.

Be patient. You'll get there just fine.

CHAPTER NINE

BRIGHT FUTURE AHEAD

*You don't decide your future.
You decide your habits, and your
habits decide your future.*
—DR. MIKE MURDOCK

My mission in this book has not been to teach you *what* to think as much as it has been to teach you *how* to think. As I've said, I believe that schools are pretty good at teaching you what to think, but they often fall short in equipping you with the mindsets and beliefs you need to thrive in your career and life after the classroom.

Thus far, I've asked you to push outside of what's conventional as you set a vision for your life (chapter 1), to silence your inner voice and the fears that hold you back (chapter 2), to adopt a series of mindsets that will drive you forward (chapter 3), and to persist despite any failures or obstacles that come your way (chapter 4).

I've encouraged you to be aware of the places where you can commit to personal growth (chapter 5), to take care of yourself so that you can keep the course on your journey (chapter 6), to personally invest in things that will endure and will benefit you down the road (chapter 7), and to keep the faith on through the winding road of life (chapter 8).

By this point, I know that you're fully equipped with the mindsets that will carry you on to become the Future You that you want to be. It won't always be easy, but nothing that's worth doing ever is.

Right now you may be thinking, *That's a lot of stuff to do! Where am I supposed to go from here?*

My advice to you is this. Just take it one day at a time, one little decision at a time. As you go, those little decisions will slowly build you into the person that you want to become. Your skills and mindsets will grow bit by bit. And at the end of your life, you'll be able to look back and see how far your adventures have taken you.

GET THE LITTLE THINGS RIGHT

In 1962, President John F. Kennedy visited NASA for the first time. During the facility tour, while walking down a hallway, Kennedy and his team passed a custodian pushing a broom. The president stopped and introduced himself to the man. After asking for his name and a few other simple questions, the president asked the custodian what he did for NASA. Without hesitation, the man proudly replied, "I'm helping put a man on the moon."

Pause and reflect on what happened there. The custodian understood something that most people struggle with: *his work was significant, and he mattered.* Keeping that building clean allowed scientists and astronauts to focus on the overall mission of putting a man on the moon. Nobody in that building had to stress about who would take out the trash or clean the bathrooms because the custodian had their backs in that department. He understood how his role was significant to the overall mission of NASA and was able to play a part in the organization's success.

Too often we believe that the little things simply do not matter. But how can anyone accomplish big goals when they aren't willing to get the little things right first?

I believe anyone can do great things, but it requires first doing little things in a great way before you can ever get there. Here are a few of the little things that I believe will help make you into the kind of person who will be capable of the great things:

HANG THE TOWEL. Life is filled with things you cannot control. So focus on controlling the things you can. For instance, remember that towel you threw on the floor instead of hanging it up where it belonged? In the big scheme of things, no big deal, right?

Would taking an extra second to hang that towel versus throwing it on the floor change your life forever? Probably not.

However, it creates the framework for long-term success habits. No change happens from a singular event. But the intentional focus to do the little things consistently will compound over time, allowing you to reach your full potential. So hang the towel. This simple act will reinforce that you are the person who does things the right way. You are not lazy, and you do not expect others to do things for you that you could do yourself.

MAKE YOUR BED. It's essential to build momentum within each of your days. The easiest way to do this is by accomplishing something early in your day. As soon as you get up, take five minutes to make your bed. Before leaving your bedroom, check out that neat-looking bed, and be proud of your work. Then move on to your next small win.

PUT THINGS BACK. Keep yourself organized, and save time and stress in the future by simply putting things back where they belong when you are done with them. You'll never have a big cleanup project when you take care of things as you go. Also, when you have a mess or clutter and cannot find things you need when you need them, your stress levels will increase, and you'll become less productive.

PICK UP THE TRASH—EVEN IF IT'S NOT YOURS. This one isn't easy because you didn't make the mess! However, if everyone took a second to pick up something they saw that shouldn't be there, the world would be a clean. If you are serious about wanting to make the world a better place, take a second to pick something up rather than just walking by.

EXPRESS GRATITUDE. You can't be hateful when you're grateful, and when you have an attitude of gratitude, you'll attract the right type of people into your life. Be thankful for everything in your life—good or bad. Remember, even when you can't yet see it, everything is happening *for* you, not *to* you.

SAY SOMETHING NICE WHEN IT'S LEAST EXPECTED. You can seek blessings from others, or you can work to be a blessing to others. Find at least one opportunity each day to say, write, or text something nice and unexpected to someone else.

SHOW UP EARLY. Time is our most precious asset. The wealthiest eighty-five-year-old in the world would trade all their wealth to return to being a fifteen-year-old again. Why? Because you can always make money, but you cannot use it to buy back time.

What does this have to do with showing up early? It's outrageously disrespectful to waste another human's time. Also, when you show up late, you silently tell other people that your time is more precious than theirs. When others show up on time and you don't, it sends all the wrong signals.

FLOSS YOUR TEETH. You only get one set of teeth and gums; take care of them. Live life maintaining attention to detail with everything. Taking just sixty seconds each day to floss your teeth will reduce your chances of tooth decay, cavities, and gum disease. There is also a connection between flossing and improved heart health. Studies show that people who floss daily live over six years longer than those who do not. Finally, taking care of your teeth and flossing will give you better breath. Who wants to be around people with horrific breath? Take care of your teeth, floss daily, let your big smile shine, and talk to people with sparkling confidence.

EXERCISE ONE EXTRA MINUTE. It's simple math: 1 extra minute each day is 7 minutes a week and 364 minutes a year. That's 6 additional hours. If you exercise for 30 minutes each day, bumping that up *to 31* minutes will add 12 extra 30-minute workouts to your year!

All these things are pretty easy to do. However, they will also seem like little things that won't matter if you skip them. But the difference between flying among the stars and being stuck on the ground is the consistent execution of the little things. The daily tasks that don't seem like a big deal are the biggest deals of all.

Anytime you are faced with a choice to do something now or take care of it later, choose the "do-it-now" road. By letting things linger, they weigh on you as they sit on your to-do list. This adds to your stress levels and holds you back from being the most productive, happiest version of yourself.

Those who accomplish big things do the little things—even if it's just for one extra minute. It's doing the little things with excellence that will make you a bigger person—a better version of yourself.

What if that custodian at NASA didn't consistently take out the trash, sweep the floors, and keep the bathrooms sparkling clean? Is it possible that the scientists, engineers, and astronauts would become upset and annoyed? And would that negative energy limit their capacity to dream bigger, more innovative ideas? And if those ideas were blocked, would we have put a man on the moon? Maybe. But maybe not.

That custodian was a big part of the NASA team. Most would overlook his role because he only did the little things. However, it's the little things that make the *biggest* difference.

MORNING ROUTINE

Building the momentum to get the little things right starts with a routine. And the first routine to master starts in the morning. Early risers get a head start in life. They accomplish goals, create plans, and build long-term foundational success habits while others sleep. As Tim Ferris says, "If you win the morning, you win the day."

My challenge to you is to determine what time you need to start your day, then wake up thirty minutes earlier. And now for the part of the book that may cause you to think I'm absolutely insane:

When your alarm goes off, don't hit Snooze. Just get up.

Yes, I realize asking a teenager to consider waking up thirty minutes earlier *and* to skip hitting the Snooze button is a radical idea. But keep in mind that this book is designed to improve your life by sharing the *cheat codes* for success used by some of the most successful adults I know in the corporate world. The decision to own those thirty minutes in the morning and become intentional with that time moves you from being average to elite.

The person you become will be determined by the number of promises you keep to yourself. Setting an alarm clock is a promise. Your feet on the floor when it wakes you is the *keeping* of that promise. Start each day with a mindset of attack, not react.

By protecting your first thirty minutes, you'll set yourself up to be able to implement the six daily disciplines, which I can promise will change your life will forever:

- Hydration
- Meditation (5 minutes)

- Positive journaling (5 minutes)
- Acts of kindness (5 minutes)
- Learning (5 minutes)
- Physical movement (10 minutes)

Remember the story of the lucky bamboo tree? These daily disciplines represent continuously watering the soil, even though nothing appears to be happening above the surface. But when your bamboo tree breaks through, it will be an amazing sight to see. So give them a try, have faith, and give it time.

STAY HYDRATED. You would think that sleeping doesn't take much work. However, your body is still active while you are off dreaming at night. When you wake up, you are dehydrated, whether you feel it or not. So as you stretch and yawn, head directly to the kitchen to grab some water. As a general rule of thumb, consistently drink half of your body weight in ounces of water each day. If you weigh 160 pounds, you'll want to consume 80 ounces of water. Start this process ASAP. Chug down as much as you can as soon as you wake up. This will help energize your body.

ENGAGE IN MEDITATION. As if I didn't already ask for enough with skipping the Snooze button, now I am going to throw meditation at you in this chapter too? Yup! I know what you immediately think when I mention meditation. You picture a monk wearing a silk robe and sitting cross-legged on top of a mountain with his palms to the sky. You're probably thinking, *There's no way I'm doing that!*

Stick with me on this one because I truly believe that meditation can be the most important five minutes of your day.

It's all about learning to be where your feet are, being present, and living within each moment throughout your day.

Today more than ever, you are living in a fast-paced, instant-answer, immediate-gratification world filled with technological stimulations and digital distractions. How do you quiet all the noise? It's a skill that is learned and developed through meditation.

As you meditate, you will have random thoughts that pop into your mind. It's natural. The goal is to be aware of the thought and recognize that it doesn't belong there at the moment. When you do this consistently, you're training your brain over time to eliminate random thoughts and distractions that pop into your head. By remaining focused and present within each moment, you'll become more efficient with your time and less stressed overall.

PRACTICE POSITIVE JOURNALING. For the next five minutes of your day, jot down every single positive thing that comes to your mind from the day before. The world sends us a disproportionate number of negative to positive stories, so spend a few minutes intentionally countering that.

The magic of this exercise is when your brain knows it will be asked to recall these positive moments first thing each morning, it then spends the day scanning the world for *more positives* and finds them in all the little things. What a blessing, right? How amazing life becomes when you constantly see all the good that surrounds you!

These little moments happen daily, and most people forget about them. The act of positive journaling will allow you to relive them the next morning, so you get twice as much joy from the experience. And when you're having some rough days and nothing seems to be going right, your positivity journal will be just the medicine you need.

PERFORM ACTS OF KINDNESS. To feel good about yourself, consistently put a smile on the face of another human. Spend the next five-minute block of your morning planning one or two things you can do to make someone else happy.

Don't let your kindness be random; make it *intentional*. Is it a text, an email, a phone call, a handwritten card, or a spontaneous visit? Is it a thoughtful gift? Or is it finding an opportunity to do something small for an unexpecting person? You decide. Use these five minutes of your morning to create a plan to bring joy to somebody's life. The more kindness you give, the more happiness you will have.

LEARN SOMETHING. If you enjoy learning by reading, spend five minutes reading a book, a blog, or an article that will improve you. If you prefer to learn by listening, spend five minutes with a podcast or audio book.

Notice the compound effect. Starting each day with just five minutes of knowledge becomes 1,825 minutes after a year or *30 hours* of lessons. Thirty hours is almost an entire workweek. Some people pay $10,000 or more to attend a weeklong seminar learning from some of the most brilliant minds on the planet. You live during such an amazing time because you can often consume the same content for free, and you don't even have to leave your house!

GET MOVING. I spent some time on this subject already in chapter 6, so I won't dive too deeply here. I will remind you that keeping your body stationary without movement is one of the worst things you can do. You may find that mornings are when you enjoy getting your full-blown daily workouts in, and that's great! However, if that's not the case, then at a minimum, you'll want to spend at least ten minutes moving and stretching your body. This could be sit-ups, push-ups, planks, basic weight lifting, stretching, yoga, or whatever else works for you.

Remember, the goal isn't perfection; it's improvement. You won't always accomplish all six of these daily disciplines. Some days you won't accomplish any. But as long as you're building the day's momentum by completing some simple tasks and stacking wins, you'll be walking with confidence as you head into whatever bigger things come next.

EVENING ROUTINE

Let's race! How about a three-mile run? First to the finish line wins. However, not everyone in this race will share the same starting line.

Those who choose to sleep in will run the full *three miles*. But those who wake up thirty minutes early and execute their six daily disciplines will start only *two miles* away from the finish line. Finally, those who also spend thirty minutes before bedtime prepping for sleep and the following day will only have to run *one mile.*

Who do you think has the best opportunity to win this three-mile race? The person who has to run the full three miles, the person who has to run two miles, or the person who only has to run one mile?

I'm guessing your money would be on the person who has to run the shortest distance, right? If so, my challenge to you in this chapter is to be the person with the one-mile race. Having a solid evening routine will set you up for success in the morning and give you a head start on your competition.

If you want to succeed in your day, you have to create a morning plan in advance—and that comes by crafting an evening routine. Let's do that now.

The first thing to do is to eliminate all unnecessary morning decisions by making those choices the night before. What will you eat for breakfast? Can you do anything to prep it in advance? Plan on working out. Choose your clothes, and lay them out. How about the clothes you'll wear to school or work? Select that outfit too. What are your lunch plans? Can you prep and pack that in advance? What are your goals for tomorrow, and what's the best first action you need to take to begin working toward them? Write those down.

You get the point. By the time most people have hit their Snooze button for the sixth time and finally drag themselves out of bed with no plan for their day, you're already dominating yours. In fact, while they are trying to find their starting line, you are already less than a mile from your finish line.

Our brains only have approximately six to eight hundred calories to burn each day. It's no different than gas in your car; you have to conserve fuel. You have to be selective with what you spend your energy on, and you can't afford to take too many wrong turns. In the morning, you'll be rested, energized, and have a full tank. This is when you'll want to be creative and do your most crucial activities.

In the evening, your tank is empty. Use this time to make simple, mundane decisions so you aren't wasting your precious morning calories on them. You should be able to whip through your basic morning decisions in the evening during a ten- to fifteen-minute window.

After completing that, it's time to prep for sleep. Sleep shouldn't be trusted to luck. Make intentional decisions thirty minutes before bed to set yourself up for success in the morning.

Here are a few basic steps.

For starters, do not eat or drink within one hour of your bedtime. As important as hydration is during the day, it's not a good idea in the evening. The goal is to get six to seven hours of quality, uninterrupted sleep. Waking up to use the bathroom will derail that plan.

Having said that, consider drinking a cup of tea before bed. When I read *The 4-Hour Work Week* by Tim Ferris, I was introduced to Yogi Soothing Caramel Bedtime tea, and it changed my sleep forever.

Use your bed for sleeping—and only sleeping. Period. Using your bed as a sofa sends your body mixed signals when it's time for sleep. But if you only use it for sleep, your body will know when you get in bed that it's time to start powering down, and you'll be able to get to sleep much faster.

And now for the big one (and I know it's the one you won't want to hear): avoid electronics—including TV—thirty minutes before your bedtime.

Think of how we put babies to sleep. We use lullabies, rocking, and bedtime stories, not TikTok videos. Screen time—whether it's a phone, iPad, computer, or TV—will stimulate your brain, which makes it more difficult to shut down for sleep.

Instead of electronics, grab a book to read before bed. Also, consider purchasing a white noise sleep machine to use instead of a television for background noise. As you lie in bed, focus on the quality of your final thoughts for the day. Count your blessings—not your problems or worries. What are you grateful for? Allow positive thoughts to occupy your head before bed!

Bookend your days with strong morning and evening routines. Eliminate unnecessary decisions in the morning by making them at night. Focus on more quality sleep. Wake up thirty minutes earlier than you normally would, and immediately execute the six daily disciplines. By becoming strategic with these two thirty-minute time blocks and deeply intentional with the actions and activities within them, you will set yourself up for major daily success. And in the big scheme of things, it's only *one hour* of the twenty-four you receive each day.

Doing things tomorrow will always be the easy option. And more often than not, you'll want to defer doing things. Especially things that are easy to do later. However, if you haven't learned by now, each crossroad essentially boils down to doing what's easy or choosing the path to *exceptional*. But you can't travel down both roads at the same time.

You are going to have tough days. You'll get to the end of those days and want to rest. And I'm not saying you shouldn't do that once in a while. But when you consistently choose that path, you'll eventually wake up in a place you don't want to be. It's then that you'll realize you have to get back to the basics:

Own the time that you can. Have a morning and evening routine. And get the little things right.

STACK WINNING DAYS

In the words of Darren Hardy, "Small, seemingly insignificant steps completed consistently over time will create a radical difference."

When it comes to establishing long-term, foundational success habits, you don't get to take the ski lift to the top. Nope. You have to take the stairs. Step… after step… after step.

Looking at all your life goals, they may seem a million miles away. If you focus on how long it will take you to climb to where you want to be, it may feel like too much. My advice is to not focus on the entire mountain ahead. Instead, focus on the only thing you can control: today.

You only get one shot at today. This specific day of the week, date of the month, and month of the year is the only such day you'll ever get. And the likelihood of you accomplishing the small, bite-sized daily goal you set for yourself today is far greater than knocking out your big, scary long-term goals. Set yourself up for success by clearly defining what a winning day looks like *today*.

All your results, good and bad, are simply a compounded total of the *small* choices you make.

Peter Drucker was known as one of the greatest minds in the field of business management. He once stated, "There is nothing so useless as doing efficiently that which should not be done at all." Those words deeply resonated with me and forced me to take a daily inventory of the things I was spending my time doing.

I share Peter's words with you so you can clearly define what a winning day looks like in your world each morning. This practice will allow you to then focus your energy on the most essential tasks and activities that will get you there.

Your success in life—however you define it—will be determined by the number of winning days you can consistently stack. If you win today, tomorrow, and the day after that, chances are you will win your week. After stacking a few winning weeks, you will have won your month. After stacking a number of winning months, you'll have won your year. Before you know it, all your winning years will have led you exactly to wherever you wanted to be. However, none of that can happen if you don't win *today* first.

If I were on my deathbed and my child at my bedside asked me if there was one thing he could do to live his best life, "Stack winning days," would be my answer.

Often people don't like to keep score of their winning days because they are scared of losing. They failure as definitive and are lured in by a scarcity mindset. The simple solution to eliminate that fear seems to be to eliminate or ignore the scoreboard. When you're tempted to do so, you are at another crossroads: *Do I keep track of and score my food choices? My fitness choices? My evening and morning routines? The execution of my six daily disciplines? What my winning day looks like?*

Choosing not to keep score is easy. But it also eliminates your ability to celebrate success and improve upon failures. Life already keeps score for you—whether or not you choose to look at it or not. You might as well make that scoreboard visible each day.

We love roller coasters. Perhaps it's the uncertainty of what is going to happen. Perhaps it's our willingness to let go of all control and just go where the next two minutes will take us. Perhaps it's the commitment to not turning back. Once we are locked in and that machine steamrolls forward, we are all in. There's no getting off.

Life is a roller coaster. But for some reason, we find the *thrills* and *surprises* less exciting. There will be climbs; there will be parts that you find exhilarating and moments when you're left breathless. You may scream and cry, but when that machine screeches to a halt, you're never upset that you locked yourself into it.

Some days you'll win. Some days you'll lose. That's just how it goes. The secret is to ride the highs for as long as you can and fight through the lows as fast as you can. But understand that both are temporary. They are intertwined, and one always leads to the other. That's just how the roller coaster of life works.

You'll have ups and downs, highs and lows, but ultimately, you only control the moments within your present day. Clearly identify what each winning day looks like, and keep your energy focused there. The more winning days you stack up, the more you'll enjoy your ride!

Only concentrate on the one thing you can control: this present day. Be where your feet are. Be present. Have faith, and follow your daily routines. Clearly define a few actions and activities you need to accomplish today, and everything beyond that will take care of itself. All the stress and uncertainty of what could happen today, as well as the fear and anxiety of what has happened in the past, make zero difference. The only thing that matters is being the best version of you today. *Just win your day.*

CHOOSE YOUR NEXT ADVENTURE

As you stand on the edge of your current journey, ready to take the next step into the unknown, it's important to remember everything you've learned along the way. Each small habit you've built, each challenge you've overcome, and every decision you've made has led you to this moment.

Every decision you've made—and every decision you will make—sends out ripples into the world, influencing not just your life but also the lives of those around you. The habits you form, the risks you take, and the paths you choose all contribute to the legacy you'll leave behind. Remember, you have limited days to live but have forever to be remembered by those you've impacted.

Think of your life as a stone thrown into a pond. The initial splash is the choice you make, and the ripples are the impact of that choice, spreading outward in ways you may not even foresee. Some ripples will be small, affecting only your immediate circle. Others will be large, touching the lives of people you may never meet. This is the power you hold—the ability to shape not just your own future but the future of the world around you.

Now the question is, *What's next?*

Life is a series of crossroads—moments where you must choose between two or more paths. These choices may seem daunting, and rightly so. The road you choose today will have a profound impact on your future. But rather than feeling overwhelmed by the possibilities, embrace the freedom they offer. You have the power to design your own adventure, to craft a life that reflects your values, passions, and dreams.

When faced with a crossroads, it's natural to fear making the wrong choice. What if you take the wrong path? What if you fail?

These are valid concerns, but remember this. The only wrong choice is the one you don't make. Indecision is a decision in itself—a choice to remain stagnant, to let fear dictate your path. Instead, choose to move forward. Choose to trust in your ability to navigate whatever comes next.

Stepping out of your comfort zone and embarking on a new adventure is never easy. It requires courage, resilience, and a willingness to embrace uncertainty. But it is in these moments—when you push beyond the familiar and into the unknown—that you truly grow. Embrace the journey ahead. Every adventure, no matter how challenging, brings with it lessons that shape you into the person you're meant to become.

In a world where it's easy to follow the crowd, there's something powerful about choosing the road less traveled. This path is often harder, filled with obstacles and fewer guarantees. Yet it's also where you'll find the greatest opportunities for self-discovery and fulfillment. By daring to be different and choosing a path that aligns with your unique vision and values, you create a life that is authentically yours.

The road less traveled is not about avoiding the mainstream for the sake of it. It's about making conscious choices that reflect who you are and what you want from life. It's about taking risks, embracing failure as a teacher, and persisting even when the journey is tough. When you look back, you'll realize that it's not the easy paths that defined you but the ones that challenged you to grow. The views from the other side of the difficulty are magnificent. Push through and see for yourself!

As you prepare to close this chapter and begin the next, take a moment to reflect on where you've been and where you want to go. The journey ahead is yours to define. Whether you choose the well-trodden path or blaze a new trail, do so with confidence, curiosity, and a sense of purpose.

Remember that every adventure—big or small—begins with a single step. It's okay if you don't have all the answers right now. What matters is that you're willing to take that step, to choose your next adventure, and to commit to the journey with all its uncertainties and rewards. The answers you seek will become clearer along the way.

Your future is not a distant destination but a journey that unfolds with every choice you make. So go ahead—choose your adventure, take that step, and see where it leads. The pen is now yours, and the following pages are blank.

It's time to choose your next adventure.

ACKNOWLEDGMENTS

First and foremost, to my incredible ride-or-die life partner, Kelly—thank you for sharing me with the world and always standing by my side, even when my goals sounded downright ridiculous. Your unwavering support and refusal to laugh (too much) when I share my audacious dreams have allowed me to spread my wings and fly. I couldn't do any of this without you.

This book is a reimagining of *Essential F-Words for Teens*, which I wrote two years ago for my son Tyler when he graduated. Now it's Conner's turn, and I'm grateful to have another opportunity to share these lessons—though I admit I'm looking forward to the four-year break before Jenna graduates. Jenna, don't worry, your book will be the best... By then, I may actually already know what I'm doing.

To my mom—I hope this proves that the hard-earned money you spent on my college journalism degree wasn't entirely wasted. It only took a few decades and a bit of trial and error, but here we are—finally putting that education to good use!

Thank you to my mentors, peers, and everyone who has contributed to my journey—whether by offering wisdom, guidance, or even a friendly nudge when I needed it most. To my team, coworkers, and friends, your encouragement fuels me, and I'm forever grateful for your belief in me.

Lastly, a special shoutout to Conner—this one's for you, buddy. Be bold, be brave, and always be YOU.

ABOUT THE AUTHOR

Scott Grates is a *USA Today* national best-selling author, TEDx speaker, entrepreneur, and trusted mentor to students and business leaders alike. With three decades of experience spanning the corporate world and the creation of multiple seven-figure businesses from scratch, Scott has developed a deep understanding of the principles that drive success. His newest book, *Think Outside the Textbook: Real Talk for Real-Life Success*, distills these principles into actionable habits to help teens confidently navigate the transition from school to the real world.

Scott's mission is personal. As a father of three, he is passionate about equipping the next generation with the tools they need to thrive in life and work. Drawing from his own journey—one marked by trial, error, and growth—Scott combines hard-earned wisdom with a relatable, approachable style. He believes that every young person deserves the opportunity to build a life of purpose, resilience, and fulfillment.

When he's not mentoring or writing, Scott hosts the popular podcast *Referrals Done Right* and travels the country to inspire audiences through his speaking engagements. Rooted in his community, Scott is a firm believer in giving back, dedicating time to mentoring students and supporting local organizations. He hopes this book becomes a compass for young readers, guiding them toward success both inside and outside the classroom.

FOR BUSINESS OWNERS
SPONSOR OR CO-SPONSOR YOUR LOCAL STUDENTS

CAREERAFTERCLASSROOM.COM

Made in the USA
Columbia, SC
05 July 2025